W9-CRA-651

MAMBUTI (PIGMY) WOMEN OF MATURE GROWTH

On the Trail of the Pigmies

An Anthropological Exploration under the
cooperation of the American Museum of
Natural History and American Universities

by

Dr. Leonard John Vanden Bergh

J.D. L.L.B.

Photographic work under the guidance of

Dr. George Burbank Shattuck

Formerly Professor of Geology at
John Hopkins and Vassar Universities

Foreword by
ROBERT H. LOWIE
Associate Curator, Department of Anthropology
American Museum of Natural History and
Lecturer in Anthropology, Columbia University

NEGRO UNIVERSITIES PRESS
NEW YORK

Originally published in 1921
by The James A. McCann Co., N.Y.

Reprinted 1969 by
Negro Universities Press
A DIVISION OF GREENWOOD PUBLISHING CORP.
NEW YORK

SBN 8371-1470-5

PRINTED IN UNITED STATES OF AMERICA

CONTENTS

ILLUSTRATIONS

PREFACE

Unlike England and Germany the United States has never colonized East Africa and this circumstance explains the relative dearth of American books dealing with that vast region. In a measure the gap is filled by Father Vandenbergh's book, which presents ethnographical observations made on the Wanyika, Wakamba, Wakikuyu, Masai, Kavirondo, and the pigmy people known as the Mambuti. A novice would not have succeeded in learning much during an eleven months' stay among half a dozen distinct groups, but Father Vandenbergh had previously spent nine years in the general region revisited in 1919 and 1920, so that he did not need to waste time on acquiring the technique of East African traveling. In addition he was aided by a practical knowledge of one of the Bantu languages.

As the author himself modestly insists, he lays no claim to being a professional anthropologist and when he presents a generalization on racial psychology or gives a casual interpretation of hereditary traits he is merely pro-

PREFACE

nouncing personal views such as may spontaneously suggest themselves to any traveler. The value of his offering—and the same might be said of not a few more pretentious publications by anthropologists themselves—lies not in the exposition of theories but in the presentation of facts recorded at first-hand or at least with the aid of competent witnesses who have had opportunities for first-hand observation.

So far as an ethnologist who is not a specialist in African ethnography can judge, Father Vandenbergh's notes on the Wanyika, Kavirondo and the Mambuti form the most valuable portion of the book. Not that his chapters on the Masai, Kikuyu and Wakamba are intrinsically of lesser interest, but merely that these tribes have already been the subject of monographic treatment, which so far as I know, does not apply to the remaining groups, so that any independent account of these latter is of proportionately greater significance.

It is a source of profound regret to scientists that the African Pigmies remain so inaccessible and accordingly so enigmatic a people. Dr. Vandenbergh's report corroborates previous accounts of their exemplary moral character from a Caucasian point of view and

PREFACE

their skill as hunters. His pictures are probably the best ever taken of members of this race. At least, so I have been told by a colleague who has himself had occasion to view Congolese Pigmies.

It may not be out of place to explain that some of the facts here described that may seem strangest to a lay reader are amply vouched for by independent authority. Thus, the avoidance of the mother-in-law noted among the Wakamba has been repeatedly reported from various Bantu groups. Indeed, the custom is widely spread among the aborigines of both Australia and North America. Similarly, the extravagant fear of defilement encountered by Father Vandenbergh in Kikuyu territory appears with equal prominence in Mr. and Mrs. Routledge's narrative. Finally, the description of Masai sexual life is paralleled, so far as essentials go, in the extensive treatises of Hollis and Merker.

With its journalistic vivacity of style and its excellent as well as ample illustrative material Father Vandenbergh's book bids fair to become a popular favorite and will doubtless stimulate interest in the natives of East Africa.

ROBERT H. LOWIE.

INTRODUCTION

THE books written on Africa in general, or on particular portions of it, are naturally short and vague in descriptive details if they are intended for purposes of scientific information dealing with ethnological data or biological, topographical or other observations. Books written on personal experiences of the travelers are mostly extravagant in descriptions of imaginary dangers and thrilling events which are rarely met with. Diaries are very dry and wearisome reading, usually to be taken with a grain of salt when it comes to personal experiences.

My own purpose in writing these chapters is to tell and give, as far as in me lies, a true version of the habits of the different tribes with which I came in contact, dwelling at length on some of the grosser customs, maybe, because they struck me as emphasizing the grade of culture, or rather lack of it, as exhibited by the tribe under discussion.

i

Looking at these peoples from this angle, I naturally did not intend to relate personal experiences among them or thrilling events which, to tell the truth, have been very few in my sojourn of ten years in Africa. But to give my friends a little detailed information, to elucidate the scope of and give more authority to matters contained in these descriptions, I might mention the object of my prolonged stay in Uganda and Kavirondo during the first nine years, from 1896 to 1905, and the last visit I made my old African friends, from the 24th of September, 1919, to the 20th of August, 1920, and how I became acquainted with their weird and often disgusting and revolting customs.

From 1896 to 1905 I was a missionary endowed with all the enthusiasm which must at all times be the underlying foundation of a missionary's career. To do my profession justice and to make my neophites worthy members of the Catholic Church, I had to go deep into their customs and traditions in order to find connecting links with which to make the transition from their former modes of living easier and more palatable.

Later on, when I returned from Africa, I found it difficult to get an unbiased or even

a credulous hearing owing to the absurd statements (absurd to my hearers) of the native
usages and habits which I spoke of. They
were true nevertheless. But to prove my
assertions I resolved to return to those parts
of Africa which seemed to supply most of the
reasons for incredulity on the part of my audiences, and this time I wished to bring back
photographs which could not lie, but which
would show to the hilt that I did not overdraw
the mark or exaggerate my findings.

The motion camera has served my purpose
well, because I find now that my pictures are
not only "amazing" and "thrilling," but, as
all the daily newspapers, such as the *Times,*
the *Globe,* etc., of New York, state, an "intelligent presentation" marked with the "stamp
of sincerity" of the man who knew what he
was going after—that was all I wished to accomplish.

The last excursion was not as full of "experiences" as my first nine years, because I
traveled quicker and with more comfort than
I did on my first trip. During the years from
'96 to '05 I always traveled on foot under the
most trying circumstances. This time I had
trains, steamboats, horses, mules, automobiles,
motorcycles and rickshaws at my command,

and consequently traveled in comparative luxury, only marching probably 500 miles in all.

The accompanying map marks the route
which my expedition took, with an approxi-
mate statement of mileage, and the mode of
transportation. I did not keep track of dates
and must only mention them from memory.
But for every custom or tradition of the following pages I can guarantee absolute truth-
fulness, suppressing rather than exaggerating
the details.

My sources of information were of the best,
where I had to consult authors or living authorities: such as the Rev. Father Wenneker
for the Wanyika of the Giliamu country; Mr.
Hobley, author of the Wakamba on the Wakamba; Sir Charles Elliott and the government reports for the Masai; the Rev. Father
Caisac of Kikuyu (than whom there is no
better authority on the Kikuyu tribe) for that
country; the Rev. Fathers Bergmans of Kisumu and Stam of Mumias for the Wakavirondo, both of whom have made a very deep
study of the Kawando tribe; and last but not
least, the Rev. Father Buyck of Kilo, Belgian
Congo, as an authority on the Mambuti Pigmies. The chapter on the Pigmies is more
or less a direct personal research, with Father

Buyck as interpreter through the medium of
a little Pygmy woman who had strayed from
the great Pygmy forest and became well acquainted with the Wanyari language, of which
Father Buyck is the best authority in the
Congo. This information is therefore first-
hand and scrupulously stated as it came to me
in answer to my prepared questionnaire and
from direct personal observation during the
time which I stayed in that district.

The journey commenced at New York,
from which harbor we sailed to Naples, in
Italy, where we took the steamship *Roma* to
Mombasa, the British East African harbor on
the Equator.

On the 26th day of November, 1919, I left
Mombasa with a sigh of relief and a radiant
desire to accomplish a feat which I had always
wished to accomplish. That feat, as I mentioned before, was more in the nature of a
justification than a thought of adventure or
potential fame and reputation. In lectures
previously given, I had often been criticized
both by my friends and members of audiences
for stretching a point or two. Even in the
course of ordinary conversation in which I
used to relate my past experiences on the
Mission field, I would notice glances of incre-

dulity exchanged between my friends, and
often felt the pangs of the braggart whose
words were doubted.

Here I had my chance to vindicate such
mortifications, because I knew that the pictures would speak for themselves and dispel
any further doubts which might arise in the
minds of those with whom I would come in
contact, for they would show the physical evidence in support of my statements. I will
admit that in the twilight of time which had
passed since these experiences I sometimes began to doubt my own memories and impressions, which might have grown in the gathering
shadows created by distance. I was therefore
impatient to set out on the long journey, which
I felt would be filled with thrills, not to be
shelved and stowed away as formerly in the
pigeonholes of my own unreliable memory, but
recorded by a scientifically certain register
which could not fail to convince where words
might leave little impression. That register
was the motion picture camera, which later
disgorged events and facts which will not only
amply justify my previous utterances, but
which will reveal to the world matters which
I had not even dared to mention before for
fear of ridicule.

Here and now I take great pleasure in expressing my grateful appreciation to Mr. Jesse Lasky, who believed me and who made it possible for me to give to the world not only these records of conditions which I hope my pictures will bring home to the civilized world—pictures which may tend to ameliorate, if not in some instances to eliminate, the hardships of the natives of Africa, and which may call attention to conditions which degrade humanity and stand in the way of happiness, and even the most elementary demands of human nature. And I would even go farther and maintain that where the commercial world would look upon this venture as a mere business enterprise, Mr. Lasky seized upon the opportunity not merely as a good commercial move for the company which he represents, but as a means to bestow a benefit on peoples who were looked upon with contempt; to promote endeavors for the uplift of these peoples; and above all, to bring home to the man in the street and the office, absorbed in business pursuits, the magnificent work which is being carried on by missionaries in the almost unknown parts of the world, and the almost superhuman acts of altruism and charity among the lepers, the lame and diseased of that dark hemisphere

of the world which has sunk away in the
shadow of forgetfulness caused by the blind-
ing luster of our sun of prosperity and by the
splendor of our social surroundings.

To see the affection and loving care bestowed
upon the forgotten element and buried stratum
of suffering negro humanity by the heroic Virgins of the Cross, known and appreciated only
by their unknown charges and protegées, to
see Sister Magdalen of Nsambya Uganda
bandaging a pestiferous leper and relieving
the agonies of a painful lupus patient, or to
see Sister Marcella of Nagalama Uganda dress
and clean the most loathsome cancer case which
medical practice has ever recorded—and all
this done with no other motive than that actu-
ating Christian charity and the alleviation of
suffering; to bring these acts of charity home
to us to enable us to assist them in their char-
itable enterprises, is a work which a moving
picture magnate has performed free of charge
at an expense which no Missionary Society
could have afforded. Nor will the scientific
world forget the revelations of great anthropological value which this series has recorded
in a lasting form, which will endure when even
such customs have been forgotten by the prog-

eny of their present devotees. For these opportunities my heartfelt thanks are due to Mr. Jesse Lasky, who gave me his complete support and confidence, and his legal counsel, Mr. Neil McCarthy, of Los Angeles, whose advice was largely, if not solely, responsible for the casting of the deciding vote in favor of the expedition.

The arrangements in Mombasa for the long saffari were not easy to plan. Caravans at the present time are not so frequent as they were in the days gone by when there was no railroad, and every one intending to travel into the interior had to do so by the saffari method. It took me two full weeks to get things in shape, and even then I had to depart without tents. "Chop boxes" were no longer to be had ready-made, as formerly, but had to be made to order; camping outfits were hard to get, and I had to assemble such things by going from one store to another. Chemical and medical supplies such as I would need were even more difficult to obtain, especially as we needed them in large quantities. For instance, when we arrived in Mombasa, the man in charge of the film developing department found that he would need cooling solutions and fixing materials which could only be had in small quantities, although they were imperatively necessary in the climatic conditions.

In the meantime, my companions were not idle. Although I did not lay much stress or take any interest in pictures outside the anthropological program which I had laid out for myself, the scenes and tropical conditions of the country were a novelty for them, the native surroundings of the people interested them greatly, although they were no novelty to me. They took pictures to their hearts' content, some of which proved to be valuable for the series which is now released. Above all, there was an interest created which paved the way for the big things ahead of us.

Personally, I suffered a great inconvenience, owing to ill health, which necessitated my being removed to the hospital on arrival in port. In Naples I had been struck down with an attack of ptomaine poisoning which had returned on board the *Roma,* which took us to Mombasa. Under proper medical care in the hospital I soon got over the effects of this malady and was ready to undertake the "big trip" in sixteen days from our arrival in Mombasa.

I might add that the tribes of which the following pages speak are the most interesting of the great variety of peoples which inhabit British East Africa and the Uganda Protectorate. Their languages vary according to the family to which the tribe under discussion belongs. The Swahili language, however, might be called the *lingua franca* of Africa, and armed with the knowledge of that tongue one may travel confident of being understood by at least the more progressive members of the larger settlements and communities. The Masai were the only exception to this rule, and into their country I took a Masai guide and interpreter who had served one of the settlers near Nairobi for a number of years as a herdsman.

Being conversant with Kiswahili, and knowing the Luganda language well, I had therefore little difficulty in communicating directly with the natives of these tribes, whilst my Baganda boys served on all occasions as splendid intermediaries when I could not get an idea across.

The itinerary of the expedition commenced from Mombasa by rail, west to Mariakani, whence we traveled about twenty-three miles north to Giliamu and back again to Mariakani to take the Uganda Railroad 200 miles west, as far as Kapiti Plains, the starting point

for Machakos in the Ukamba country, 28 miles
northwest. Thence we traveled by motor car
to Nairobi for 60 miles southwest. From·
Nairobi 40 miles north to Chaina Falls, 10
miles' marching distance from the Mangu Mission in Kikuyu. To visit the Masai we returned to Nairobi, traveling 60 miles south
from there by motor car and on foot to
Nguruya's Masai settlement. Returning to
Nairobi again, we took the train to Kisumu, on
the Victoria Nyanza, the center of the Kavirondo country, where we visited the north and
southern portions in different parties, going
south to Kisi, a distance of 50 miles, by boat
and on foot, and north in a circle to Mumias
and Kakamega, a route of some 150 miles on
foot and by motor car.

Leaving Kisumu we took the *Winifred* to
Kampala Uganda across the Victoria Nyanza,
where we took some wonderful pictures of the
Baganda. Going east 80 miles to Jinja, we
started down the Nile toward the Kyoga Lake
(a distance of some 70 miles), after crossing
which we traveled on land toward the Albert
Nyanza, a matter of 100 miles, partly on foot,
partly on a motor truck, to Butyaba, where we
caught a boat to Mahagi in the Congo.

Here we were in poor luck, having to march

the whole distance to the Wanyari village of
Zabu, some 200 miles, all the way on foot, with
an occasional lift in a hammock, and back
again to Kasenyi, returning to Butyaba,
whence we took a boat to Nimuli. In order
to avoid the Fola Rapids, we had to march
again for a distance of 100 miles to Rajaff,
whence we followed the Nile in uninterrupted
comfort of Nile steamers and railroad cars.

It is a peculiar coincidence that the elevation at Jinja (the source of the Nile) is 3,641
feet, whilst the distance from Jinja to Alexandria is 3,642 miles, allowing the Nile one
foot average drop from its origin to its flow
into the Mediterranean.

The climate varies with the districts one
visits, as does the temperature. For instance,
the average temperature in Kikuyu in and
around Nairobi would be little over 75 degrees,
while in Karthum in the Soudan, the ther-
mometer hovers between 120 and 112 degrees
all the year round; whilst the hot winds blow-
ing from the great desert make living conditions unbearable.

The title of this book is more or less mis-
leading, there being only one chapter on the
Pigmies. But owing to the fact that there is
little to say about the Congo dwarfs whose

history is not only vague but communication with whom is extremely difficult to establish; and, moreover, since the other tribes spoken of in these pages are scattered on the way to the Congo, "The Trail" seemed to explain the underlying motive better than any other term.

DR. LEONARD JOHN VANDEN BERGH

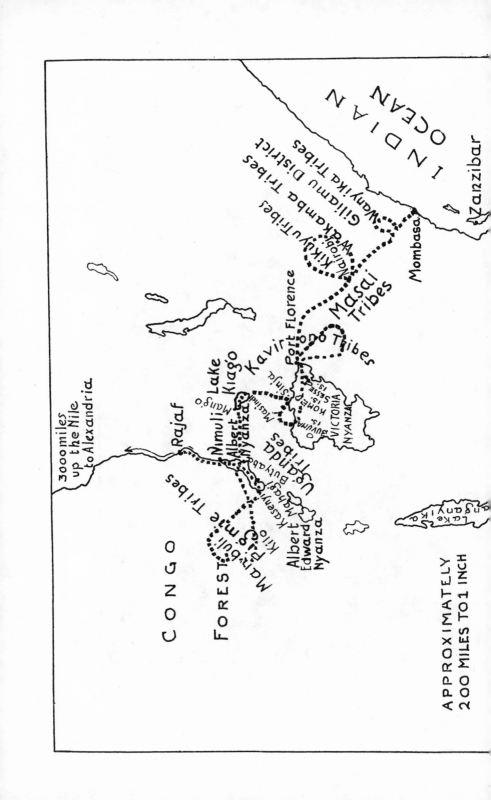

THE WANYIKA

In order to get a good start without taking undue chances I took the party to a country and a tribe new to me to get the technical procedure in good running condition without jeopardizing the pictures which would form part of the main issue. This initiation proved to be very valuable in so far as we happened upon a few points which were of great interest to the comparative tribal studies which I was about to make. And it happened in so unexpected a manner that it is well worth relating.

On the eve of Thanksgiving Day, 1919, Father Wenneker of the Giliamu Mission had sent me his mule to lessen the fatigue of the long twenty-mile march from Mariakani Station to Giliamu. Just about sunset I passed a party of dancers, whose singing, with the accompaniment of the tinkling of innumerable bells, made my charger restive. I tried to steer him into the midst of the dancing party, but failed miserably until I whipped him in

1

that direction. A great shout went up from the hundred throats and more of a savage mob, and the mule reared and snorted and bucked to such an extent that my attention was no longer riveted on the wriggling mass and their awe-inspiring bell "jazz." Presently a boy, well dressed in khaki, jumped from the ranks of the onlookers and calling the mule by his pet name took hold of the bridle and made an attempt to calm my shivering mount.

"Beast afraid, sir," he said; "me speak English very good. You go Mission?"

"Right-o," I replied; "but I want to see this dance first. What's all the row about?"

"He dance dead man."

"Do they dance at funerals?" I asked.

"Yes," he replied; "but dead man no here— to-morrow other dance there."

And he stretched out his hand toward the north.

That settled the question in my mind, and turning the mule's head, I went toward the Mission. The boy followed me and I engaged him in conversation, which led to the arrangement whereby he agreed to take me to the next dance on the following day.

We took our motion camera and what we snapped there will become a record of

Wanyika history which will be well worth preserving in the archives of ethnology. With a little bribe, handed out with discretion to the leaders of the dance, we got a complete program of a dance which has a deep meaning in its weird movements and wailing songs; it portrays a great fear of the spirits and a profound expression of passionate sexual desire. For this reason I repeat here what I learned there.

The Wanyika occupy a stretch of country approximately forty miles square, extending from Mazeras to Ukamba station. This territory is not inhabited exclusively by the Wanyika, for there are other tribes within the boundaries, and parts of tribes calling themselves distinctive names like Wagiliama and Wakamba. The exact origin of the Wanyika, like the genesis of most tribes, is difficult to ascertain definitely, and an examination of the legendary ancestry of these people would lead us far afield.

The men have no distinctive dress, but when they deign to affect clothes they adopt the fashion of the Swahilis. Ivory rings adorn their arms above the elbow and variegated beads and wires about the neck and arms complete the costume. The girls wear a less strik-

ing chain with fringes, which serves as a laval-
lière. The pendants are of copper and brass,
being in effect chains of one-half to an inch in
length.

The Wanyika are distinctly agricultural,
and they live principally on maize, mohogo
(arrow-root), a small bean known as "podjo,"
ground nuts and cocoanuts, mawele and ma-
wimbi. All of these edibles are grains. Most
of the cultivation is done by the women with
a minimum of assistance from the men. One
may not speak of "the weaker sex" with reference to the Wanyika women—or, for that matter, with reference to many other African
women—for it is not uncommon to find women
serving as *bapagazi* (porters) on short saf-
faries. Europeans hesitate to employ women
on long journeys, but on a saffari of fifteen or
twenty miles there generally is a majority of
female porters. I was surprised on arriving
at the station of Mariakani to find that of the
fifty porters for whom we had previously contracted, twenty-eight were women, the remainder being men and small boys.

As I have suggested, the food and drink of
the Wanyika are primitive. Their chief diet is
the mohogo or Manioc root, which may be consumed raw or cooked. This root is cultivated

extensively and comes to maturity within five months after planting. It is a nutritious food and it builds up strength to a surprising extent. The second staple is maize (corn), which is not so common and is confined to certain districts. Maize is prepared either in a mortar and pestle or milled in grinding stones. These stones are operated by hand, of course, the nearest approach to machinery being a set of milling stones engineered by two girls. Maize is a delicacy and receives careful treatment from the native cooks. It may be baked in ashes or boiled on the cob, as at our own Coney Island.

On our way to the dance, I saw a man sitting on the ground, directing a couple of women in rooting up mohogo (arrow-root). It reminded me of an experience of twenty-three years ago, when I had quenched an overpowering thirst by the same process which these women were following. We dug up the roots so that we might suck what little juice there was in them, and well do I remember the ensuing gastric fever with which the drink afflicted my old friend, Bishop Biermans. I was curious to see what the Wanyika would do—and the picture I had taken showed that this gray-headed son of the equator repeated the action of my old friend, and ate the root raw. But I doubt whether he suffered any evil effects from it, like my buddy of 1896.

Large sweet potatoes are ubiquitous and popular, but beans are not so plentiful and they serve as a manner of side dish. To vary the Wanyika menu, there may be cocoanuts, ground nuts, pembe (a small barley-like grain), and the papali and the mango. The last two are fruits and are sought after to sell rather than to eat. Cocoanut water is a staple refreshment after a fatiguing saffari.

The Wanyika may be considered vegetarians, for meat is expensive. Cattle are money among the Wanyika, and they prefer to save their cattle to barter for a higher order of chattel (in their eyes)—women. Goats and sheep and fowl are seldom killed, for they constitute the personal wealth of the natives.

When we arrived at Giliamu, on the eve of Thanksgiving day, I was surprised to hear a gobbler honking in the backyard. I turned to Dr. Shattuck.

"What does this suggest to you on this of all days?" I inquired.

"It reminds me of what is going on in Poughkeepsie at this very moment," he replied.

"Why not here," I suggested, "when the wherewithal is calling for the occasion?"

I asked the good Father if he could let us have a turkey, and picking this gobbler as a progressive—and therefore young—because he was so noisy, I gave my cook, Simoni, orders to catch him.

Next morning we left for a good day's work, and the funeral dance expelled all further thought of Thanksgiving until the big fellow was placed before me. His size made me doubt his youth, and the first bite on a slice of white meat confirmed my suspicions. He must have been an old sheik, and before my departure I realized that two mouthfuls of turkey had cost me six dollars apiece.

A young pig also made me think that after all the high cost of living in New York did not compete with the prices at the Giliamu mission; but then I did not know that the turkey and the pig were importations designed to introduce the breed on this unpromising soil.

Cocoanut water and milk are important beverages, but the national drink is a concoction which differs from the ordinary native "home brew." This drink is the palm wine, which brews itself over night. The palm tree from which they tap this precious fluid has widespreading branches with a small crown on each. This crown is removed and the tip thus bared is cut during the early part of the day and is tapped in the evening. This is a simple and effective brewing process. The tip being scraped to open the pores, the wine seeps through to the tip, where it is caught in a cup. The juice is protected from the sun by a little piece of matting placed over the tip, which prevents the liquid from drying up. The natives relish palm wine, but I doubt whether any white men—even the most extreme anti-prohibitionists—will enjoy it. To my palate it seemed like pig's wash—but the natives imbibe it copiously and become hopelessly and unmanageably inebriated on their "liquor." I discovered this natural distillery quite by accident.

Lounging around, on the first Sunday, in a camp chair on the veranda of the mission, I noticed a movement on the limb of a tree in the distance. My curiosity was aroused, and I made for the tree—and what I saw there was a novelty to me. I had heard of, seen and tasted different native brews of wine or beer, but this was a new one in my catalogue. The being moving in the palm tree—I thought at first that it was a chimpanzee—was a boy sitting astride a limb. He had a hatchet in his hand, and a pointed calabash the size of a quart bottle protruded from the end of the limb on which he sat. I watched him carve the top of the limb and learned that a juice flowed out of the bleeding branch—palm wine. I have since seen many such surgical operations performed on palm trees, but I cannot share in the enjoyment of the fluid which makes the Wanyika so lugubriously and sometimes so maudlinly happy.

Wanyika huts are anything but elaborate. Even the palaces of the chiefs are tawdry apologies for houses. The picture on the following page offers a fair illustration of the average Wanyika dwelling. The huts are built of *budongo* (adobe), or grass, or consist merely of a straight thatched roofing which extends to the ground. The framework is composed of the straightest available sticks tied horizontally to a few thicker rods placed in the ground from four to five feet apart. This framework is made in duplicate so that the builder may fill in the distance between the two frames with grass or adobe.

The roof is supported by two tall posts, from which the main rafter hangs, and from this rafter the smaller rafters are tied diagonally to the top of the walls. Cross sticks are used to make the surface of the roof strong enough to bear the weight of the crowning thatch, which represents the greatest artistic feat involved in the building of the hut. It takes an experienced hand to place the grass evenly on the roof so that the distribution of weight is uniform throughout. The grass remains in place by its own weight, except over the main center rafter, where it is fastened with grass ropes. A small "veranda" juts out above the walls to protect them from rain. In the ordinary hut, which looks like a big round basket turned upside down, this precaution is unnecessary, and the average native prefers the "basket" pattern because it is easier to build.

There is only one opening in the hut, a four-foot incision which serves as a door, windows and chimney, all in one. It is only two feet six inches wide, so that entry into the hut is accomplished only by a squirming process. There is little light in the huts, and the atmosphere is intolerable, for the hut shelters not only human beings, who are unpleasantly fragrant, but chickens, goats, sheep, and not infrequently a few calves.

Cattle come first, the wives second. The

reason is that it takes cattle to buy wives with, and once the wife is bought she'll keep herself, but cattle have to be petted and cared for lest they be lost. That seems to be the train of thought in the native mind all over Africa. They give more care to a sick calf than to a sick wife. Hence the great care they bestow on a kraal, or cattle pen. Barring the absence of a roof, the enclosures sheltering the cows are better built than their own huts. A young calf is kept in the hut and occupies the center of the family's domicile. Even bellowing at night seems to be music to the native ear.

There is no furniture in the house except a few water jars, two or three *endekos* (gourds), a stone tripod for the cooking pot, and the paraphernalia for grinding corn, which includes a mortar and pestle. Only the most civilized natives indulge in bedsteads and mats, for the majority sleep on the floor without coverings of any sort.

Sometimes the hut is partitioned to allow privacy for husband and wife. Two other partitions are made under the roof to act as a granary, and a third is constructed as a basket or vat for palm wine. So the "living height" of the hut is cut down to four or five feet— and the limitations of space, combined with the odors of humans, beasts and the cuisines, make the huts uninhabitable for one accustomed to the niceties of white ventilation.

We had a bad day on the first of December, having marched out for a distance of ten miles from the mission to the Giliamu government headquarters. We found our trip wasted, and the only picture we had taken was that of an Indian store, the proprietor of which was kind enough to offer us some tea. We had scarcely left the "bazaar" when a characteristic African rainstorm put the climax on a miserable day with a terrific shower, which fortunately overtook us close to a small native village. My boy had the foresight to bring an umbrella with him—more for sunshade than rain—but it kept me dry from the knees up until we arrived at the village, where the chief offered us shelter. And such a shelter!

There were a dozen of us packed into the hut. Dr. Shattuck and I were crammed in with our boys, porters and the chief's staff. The odor was terrific. The rats scurried between my feet and climbed up the thatch immediately behind me. I'd rather face a lion or a snake than a rat—any time. I was sitting on the edge of a bedstead manufactured of four slender sticks stuck in the ground and topped with other smaller sticks arranged crosswise and covered with a hard cowhide. One end reached the sloping roof, being partly stuck in the thatch. When a rat approached I moved to the far side of the bedstead, and here I had the pleasant sensation of dirty water seeping through the thatched roof, trickling down my neck. I moved back to my original position, and presently I heard the scratching of the rat scurrying along the cowhide bed-top that drove me off my seat with a start which made me bump into a rafter of the hut with an impact that left a black bruise on my forehead. I left the hut, and with my boy holding the umbrella, reinforced with a blanket over my head, I spent the best part of an hour under a tree, which if it did not keep me dry at least kept me away from the rats.

Wanyika mats and pottery are poor exhibits. The Wanyika confine their pottery activities to the making of the *nsua* or water-jar. A half-grown cocoanut hollowed out and mounted on a stick is their only cup. Their mats are extremely crude and scarce. Most of the families are without mats and only the minority can boast this adjunct of civilization.

The villages of the Wanyika are very small and confine themselves entirely to the huts of one family. The father or the older brother is the chief of this little village and he knows no superior, for the Wanyika are not inclined toward the feudal system. Consequently the colonies are small.

Usually there is a little stockade for cattle—if the chief owns any—which forms the center of the village. If the head of the family has more than one wife he builds a separate hut for each partner and the children of each wife live with their mother. Sometimes the village is surrounded by a low hedge of thornbushes or by other growths which serve as a barricade. Where the head of the family happens also to be chief of some other families, a small space is cleared around the main hut. Here tribal consultations take place and family brawls are adjudicated.

The plantations are close to the villages and occupy as little ground as is absolutely necessary for the upkeep of the family. The result of this economy is frequently disastrous, for a famine invariably finds the natives without reserve stores, and as the natives do not sell food to the members of their own tribes, famine brings wholesale starvation with it.

It occurs to the traveler through the province of Giliamu that it is a great pity that a country so well adapted for cultivation and so luxurious in its wild growths of all sorts of trees and grasses should not inspire the natives to be more provident and more industrious. They could make this country a wonderfully productive land if they had the stamina and the inclination to work and to produce. It is another example of the lack of distribution in nature and the need of opportunity. Were this a white man's country, fortunes could be made by progressive farmers, and there would be a market for the staples of foreign countries. All facilities are there. Cattle fatten on the bare land with its deep carpet of rich nutritious grasses and herbs—yet the herds of cattle are small and far between.

Physically, the natives are strong and muscular. They are of average height, although the women are likely to be undersized. Their mental development is low and their intelligence even below the standard of the average African tribe. They are listless and very hard to move. They are sullen and disinclined to respond to a question even if it be for their own benefit.

They are neither fish, flesh nor even good red herring so far as their morals are concerned. I should describe them as laissez-faire moral-

ists—or unmoral.   There is a certain sense of
shame attached to the birth of illegitimate children, but they overcome this obstacle to the
free indulgence of their passions by preventive
measures and abortive remedies.   Prostitu-
tion, as such, is not known to them, but when
a famine arrives, the women leave for the coast
and easily become victims of their craving for
food, selling themselves in the open market to
the highest bidder.   The dances, of which I
shall have more to say presently, are not con-
ducive to pure thoughts and in these dances
there are movements which arouse sexual im-
pulses not easily to be checked—especially
among the girls, who are of that age "where
brook and river meet."

The Wanyika girls marry just as they are
coming to maturity and as an argument for
their virtue it may be said that they usually become mothers in the regular course of time.
This fact leads to the inference that the girls do
not over-indulge before their marriage, although it would not be scientifically correct to
say that all of them are virgins before marriage, like the Kavirondo, for instance.

As mothers, they are careful of their children and seem to have a well-developed ma-

ternal instinct. They attend to their babies
until the time for weaning and treat them ten-
derly, even decking them out bravely with
beads from their own slender store. They
carry the little ones on their backs, often without artificial support, and it is curious to see
the babies cling to their mothers with the
tenacity of a little monkey. (At feeding time,
the mother swings the baby around on her
hip by one arm and gives it the breast while
the child hangs on to its parent with its tiny
legs as it rests on the hip, where it is supported
by the mother's arm.)

Losing a baby through neglect is a crime
that a father never forgives his wife and consequently the poor woman must carry it day
and night in the village, on the road and in the
field. For this purpose they carry the per-
ambulator and cradle on their backs in the
form of a sack fastened around the waist under the arms, supported with a sling from the
head. To the father the baby means a future
helper in war as a boy or advancement in the
community in the girl for whose sale in marriage he realizes cattle and goats.

The one safeguard of the morality of unmarried girls is the fear of their fathers, who

look upon their daughters as prospective
sources of wealth. Consequently, when the
girls become mothers of illegitimate children,
their market value declines and the fathers
have their own methods of revenging themselves. If the lover happens to become the
husband, however, the "value" of the girl is
not affected.

Marriage takes place at the age of fourteen
or fifteen, depending on the maturity of the
girl, who, at this time, is only an apprentice in
cooking and other household arts and who is
therefore taken into the home of a sister or
the mother of the bridegroom for further instruction. Her love, of course, is not deep-
rooted, and it is chiefly subservient, the fear
of her husband dominating her affection. She
takes matters for granted and follows "the
natural course" as she has learned it from her
mother. When, however, incompatibility of
temperament becomes too evident, the girl
leaves her husband and the father must return
the price which the girl has brought him.
When the husband dies, the older brother of
the deceased inherits the wife, who becomes his
property outright; but in case of divorce, the
older brother cannot recover the purchase

JUNGLE HOME SWEET HOME

VILLAGE LIFE

Village council in Giliamu   Evening meal in Uganda

Native store in Giliamu

price paid by the first husband. Under such circumstances, the older brother usually receives another female of the family to replace the deserter.

Polygamy is the universal system, and a man may have as many wives as he can afford to buy. But the prevailing poverty, due to the scarcity of cattle and the lack of industrial enterprise, forces most men to be content with one wife.

Joseph, my guide to the dance, confided to me, with a broad smile on his homely features, that he was about to marry, and with commercial shrewdness he dwelt especially on the high cost of living—of wives, I might say. He suggested that it was the greatest pleasure of his life to assist me as interpreter, but that the loss of time postponed the wedding for as many days as he was at my service, because he could earn no money and buy no cattle so long as he was with me. I asked him how many head of cattle he was short. "One," he replied, and seeing my opportunity, I made a bargain with him. I was to give him the price of the beast if he would let me be a witness to his marriage and permit me to photograph the event. He beamed with delight at the offer, and before my departure I saw Joseph the happy owner and husband of as charming a little dusky lady as I met on my long journey.

The possessor of two wives is looked upon as a rich man, and the owner of more is considered a capitalist. I have heard of one great mogul who owns sixty wives, and he is the Crœsus of the tribe. Once the purchase price is agreed on and a deposit paid to bind the contract there is little objection on the part of the father to clandestine meetings of the future husband and wife, and the bridegroom-to-be is ever a welcome guest.

Wives take great pride in presenting their lords with as many descendants as possible, and families of four or five are the average. The childless wife is in ill-repute whether or no it be her fault. At childbirth the wives are assisted by the older women of the neighborhood, but the local midwifery is crude and the results are obvious from the appearance (enlarged navel) of many of the natives.

From a standpoint of culture I am always interested in finding out whether a tribe is endogamic or exogamous. Endogamy, or in-marrying, traditions are naturally a manifestation that the tribe is of low standard in the scale of culture, because when they marry in the same clan they naturally are trespassing a first law of nature which finds its own downfall in the end. Marrying outside the clan according to a certain law prohibiting even intermarriages between relatives down to the fourth generation will give a clan or tribe a chance to proper out-breeding to preserve the race in healthy condition.

Wanyika marriages are entirely exogamous. There is no intermarriage inside the clans, and the men choose their wives from outside families to protect the purity of the breeding. There are different ways of identifying families, the principal one being identification by the name given at birth. I have been unable to find any totem system, but the traditions of the family are guarded carefully.

Venereal diseases are not common among the Wanyika, as one may gather from the freedom with which they expose their bodies. The women wear little more than a short kilt and leave the upper parts of their bodies entirely exposed, and of the thousands of natives we saw, there was only one case in which the ravages of syphilis were plainly visible. We took a picture of the victim to show the scarcity of the disease.

The women mature—or, better, age—

rapidly. This condition may be explained by the fact that life is all work and no play for them, and that continuous child-bearing tends to make them old before their time. The men, spending their lives, "dolce far niente," retain their youth admirably, so that men twice the age of some women are strong and well-preserved when the women are long since worn out and done with active participation in the life about them.

The Wanyika marriage ceremony is about the most cold-blooded commercial transaction that I have yet found among the native tribes of Africa. Possibly there is a certain amount of love and affection involved as far as the man and his wife are concerned, but the parts which the parents of the bride play savor of the straight bargain and sale across the counter. You pick your article, ask the price, haggle until an agreement is reached—and the sale is then and there completed.

The wedding which I witnessed was that of a well-educated young Munyika who had been a postman in the Cape and who finally returned to his own tribe because of his great affection for his own people. He returned with a little bankroll—which became known to the natives. After looking about for a bride

he finally settled his choice on a young maiden
with whom he came to a private understanding. When the day for his application to the
girl's father arrived, he entered the courtyard
of his future parent in an ecstatic frame of
mind. The father was home and had been
acquainted with the fact that his daughter's
affections were taken up entirely by young
Mwangari, who was a "likely" son-in-law and
a good source of revenue for Mwamkare, the
old man. There was little argument in the
matter. As soon as the father had heard the
declarations of the lad, he summoned the girl
out of the hut, where she was waiting anx-
iously. He asked her whether she cared for
Mwangari, and Kaïdza answered that she
worshiped the ground he trod on and that she
would follow him wherever he might lead.
With an imperious motion of the hand,
Mwamkare waved her back to the hut. Then
began the customary bargaining—the close,
relentless bargaining that only a Wanyika
father seems to be able to indulge in.

"If you are enamored of the girl," he said
to the young lover, "you are showing good
taste, because she is one of the prettiest girls
of the tribe, if not the most beautiful of all.
I have always set great store by this girl, and

I always knew that some day she would bring me a good price. Now—I shall let you marry her if you pay me eight cows and twenty-five jars of palm wine for her."

Mwangari was taken aback and told the father that he had been to a foreign country where matters were reversed, and that he had learned to cherish a wife according to the European code, which forbade a man to let his wife labor on a plantation.

"She will lead the life of a lady," he pleaded, "and all that she will have to do will be to cook the food which I shall buy for her."

The father, however, insisted on his price, and settled the bargain on his own terms, for Mwangari feared that Kaïdza might think that he underestimated her value. His chivalry was not emulated by the father, who held out for his price to the last pound of beef, as it were. Later Mwamkare sent his oldest son to inspect the cattle, which might later serve as the purchase price of a wife for himself.

On the return of the son and his approval of the cattle hung the consummation of the bargain. The boy returned with a satisfactory report, and the agreement was made. Mwangari thereupon went home to his sister's hut and told her to prepare to receive his bride.

The next day he returned to the village of his prospective father-in-law and brought with him a few pieces of wearing apparel such as the young girl had never dreamed of. After paying the first installment of five jars of palm wine to Mwamkare, the boy took his wife without further ceremony to his sister's hut, where she was installed not only as a guest but as the wife of the head of the family and treated with proper deference.

This primitive, cold transaction is much more barbarous than, for instance, the manner in which two Baganda marry. I shall discuss the Baganda wedding later on, but here I may add to one who takes an interest in the Wanyika, the mercenary marriage is a disheartening institution.

Wanyika women celebrate festal occasions like weddings by drinking to the point of inebriation, but they do not smoke, snuff or use tobacco. The men enjoy snuff not only as it is used by more civilized races, but as a "chew." As I have pointed out, the natives are addicted to stimulants, but here again poverty is the mother of continence. Their lack of resources prevents much indulgence in their pet vices.

There are but few tribal marks among the Wanyika. Some natives, especially among

the younger generations, have none at all.
Others have the two lower center front teeth
removed and the corresponding upper teeth
filed in the form of an inverted V. They
pierce the ears, but the aperture never is
greater than the width of one of our five-cent
pieces. At the age of three, boys are circumcised, and at the age of eight, the dental operations referred to above are made. But the
markings, which are a form of crude paganism, seem to be dying out in the present generation.

Superstition and forms of idolatry are extremely interesting to me, and there is a variety of these practices in Africa which is
astounding. Sun, moon and star worshipers,
which the natives all are to a certain extent,
are to me the most logical phenomena in
Africa. Realizing that there is no mode of
lighting up at night, they naturally would welcome the dawning sun in the morning, which
comes to them as a redeemer to expel all the
terrors and dangers of darkness, or the moon,
which enables them to at least go outside their
huts without being pounced upon by some
wild beast which may be hiding within arm's
reach. In the early days of 1896, when I first
touched African soil, and I saw the porters in

the caravan offering incense on their little
amulet pallets to a new crescent moon, I
thought the worship foolish; but now, knowing the danger of the night through a long experience, it looks to me like the most logical
thing for them to do to hail the coming of
light the savior. Other systems, of course, are
stupid and silly, and in a great many cases
harmful, but even there some extenuation of
their traditions can always be found.

The Wanyika have little superstition or
idolatry, although there are certain animals
which are sacred and immune from slaughter.
The chief object of this immunity is the hyena,
which is never molested, and whenever a black
calf is born the natives cover its head with a
box, tie the helpless animal to a tree and offer
it as a sacrifice to the first hyena which may
find it.

The spirits of the ancestors and of persons
who have died recently are fed according to
the primitive animistic ritual. The Wanyika
dig a hole in the ground and place half a gourd
in it. They pour cocoanut milk in the gourd,
mixing it with water, adding some food, such
as flour or meat, and leave the offering for the
nourishment of the departed spirit. The spirit
is summoned by a series of incantations. Only

those who were respected are honored with this ceremony and with the funeral dance, which I shall describe presently. Others are merely placed in the ground in front of the hut, to pass forever out of memory.

On our way up to Giliamu we had an opportunity to observe a dance which was being indulged in by the Wanyika, and in which we found that only men participated. There was a chorus of about a hundred children, ranging from ten to fifteen years in age, some of whom were girls. However, there is a dance, known as the *matanga,* in which both sexes take part. This is the funeral dance, which is done only when a member of the tribe has died. It is attended by ceremonies designed to expel evil spirits. First, a white cloth flag is placed on a stick at the hut of the departed tribesman. In the dance, the leading dancer wears a red sash about his waist, to which a spiritual significance is attached. This man works himself into a frenzy, until he finally runs wild in the semicircle of the dancers, and after making fearful grimaces and performing astounding antics, he finishes the dance with a wild leap in the air. In this last evolution he holds the sash and places a straight kick in the stomach

THE FUNERAL DANCE

The Wanyika wear a bell harness on the right leg at a funeral dance.

ADMINISTERING JUSTICE

Ordeal in Ukamba called Kithito.

Uganda trial. The winning party rolls his thanks in the dust at the judges feet

of the imaginary evil spirit to drive him for all time from the premises.

The first dance which we saw was most fantastic. The men were divided into three classes of dancers. The first and largest class wore a legging on one leg, composed of bells very similar to our sleighbells, fitted on strips of rawhide which form a harness bound tightly around the right leg from ankle to hip. They move the leg provided with this ringing apparatus at a given cadence of singing, which is done by the choir of children. The second section of dancers runs around like so many demons through the onlookers and dancers, jumping high every now and then with a weird shout, while they shake their heads as though they would rise higher—or as though they had been stung by an electric shock. They wear a headdress of long, flowing monkey skins, and carry a wand in the right hand, which they shake at intervals as though attacking an invisible enemy.

There are leaders who act as "majores domi," with authority to direct and to bring into line those who seem about to fall out. These also carry whips with which they drive off the too inquisitive spectators who might interfere with the gyrations of the dancers and with which they keep the dancers in order. The dance moves sidewise, bearing to the right with a slow and graceful movement. The dancers keep time with the music so well that one cannot refrain from applause at the conclusion of the performance. The music supplied by many little children's voices gives an air of naïve innocence to the dance, and the youngsters stand together as they sing, with their hands on one another's shoulders, moving on four abreast, with just a hint of swaying.

The dancers evidently are picked members of the tribe, for they are conscious of the honor bestowed upon them, and move without a false step. While the trained dancers were going through their movements, a band of young men were going through the same evolutions, being guided by the master dancer, who ordered them about like a drill sergeant. These novices would glance at the "professionals" whenever there was an opening through which they could watch them.

They looked on with that hungry ambition which seemed to say, "Wait till I get in that line!" They had to practice almost against the music, for whenever a "faux pas" occurred the step was repeated, regardless of the rhythms supplied by the children. And the most curious feature of the ceremony was that there was not a woman participating or looking on in the crowd of at least thiee hundred persons.

The Wanyika begin their training for this dance at an early age, for I found that even youngsters of five or six are trained religiously to become members of the guild from which the "professional" dancers are selected. In the place of the gaudy leg chains which form the principal decoration of the older dancers, the children have a poor substitute in the shape of a chain made of mango stones which are strung on a bit of copra and wound around the lower part of the leg with one loop fixed about the big toe and the other tied about the calf. It is not much of an imitation of the real thing, but it keeps the youngsters lively and in good trim. The more they wriggle their legs, the better they seem to keep time, and they seem to enjoy their performance as though it were their life's task. The dancing teacher also seems to relish his duties, for he acts in a whole-hearted manner, as though he were dancing with his equals. His standards with the children seem to be fully as rigid as though he were teaching a group of professionals.

Girls are permitted to participate in the dance of the boys. At first they are obviously coy and bashful, as though they were on forbidden ground, but once the dance is in full swing they have to be restrained from making advances to the young lads. They make a striking effect with their thin calico skirts, which have double or triple fringes, according to the wealth of the girl's family. These concessions to modesty are from three to nine inches in length and do not extend far down the thigh. Beyond the swaying skirt, the girls are not particular about their costumes, for they are rather fond of exhibiting the pretty figures to which many of them lay claim.

The funeral dance, of which I saw a sample on the 29th of November, was a revelation and raised the Wanyika in my estimation. Why they should thus mourn their dead is still a puzzle to me, but the dance brings out some of the most artistic evolutions that I have ever seen. The graceful, rhythmic swaying of the men's bodies is marvelous, well studied and carefully executed. The same rattling harness described previously is worn at the funeral dance, and part of the dancing is the same so far as the men are concerned. The novel addition is the wiggling and wriggling—I cannot define it otherwise—of the couples when they meet for a set. It may sound curious to the American mind, but it is only in harmony with the native customs all over Africa that the women do the calling here, showing that the woman is the slave, always catering to man, her master.

The sets, of which there may be two or three, are made up of picked male dancers, all tall and well-built men, and girls of from twelve to sixteen, whose wool-topped heads barely reach the chins of their partners. The men sing a weird song, telling of the sad death of the subject of the "wake," and ask the girls to join them in bewailing the sad departure, reminding them that when a person dies there must be a substitute to replace the deceased, lest the tribe perish. In answer to these tactful overtures the girls glance at one another coyly and diffidently from their place, which is about fifty feet removed from the line of men. The men resume their exhortations and the maidens walk up to the line of men. They do not speak on their arrival and make only the slightest courtesy, after which they return to their previous position.

The men then begin a snake-like motion of the body, and with two taps of the armored leg for every one of the unadorned mate, they advance toward the women, with all the benefits to be derived from the jingling of the bells. Approaching the line of maidens, the men allure the fair ones with a most intriguing execution of a most captivating pass, after which each faces a partner, who bows a bashful assent to the invitation. Thereupon the man lays his chin on his partner's forehead. Each begins a motion of the body which is rather suggestive, but the situation is not so shocking as it might be, for both keep their hands hanging limply at their sides and bend forward. The crowd looks on and claps hands in applause, at the same time singing a crude but effective ditty. The "tout ensemble" is a wonderful display of native art carried out in the minutest detail, as though a ballet master had spent years in training the performers. But there is no stage director among the Wanyika, no miracle man of æsthetics. Each native teaches the next what he knows, and those whose execution is not up to the standard are barred from the dance. Perhaps this description gives the impression that the dance is monotonous, but I could watch the evolutions for hours and always find new features of interest.

The final act, when the mixed dancing is completed, is a wild scene. The dancers take leave of the maidens and withdraw to a position about twenty feet away, where they start a war dance in a semicircle, all walking or dancing slowly toward the right, stamping their armored legs. When they have assumed their formal position, one member jumps out of line and runs around the semicircle, swaying his hands and feet. Another reproduces his antics, and then the scene is set for the master dancer, who comes out solemnly and takes the front of the stage. This official leaps about and runs the circle until he is "warmed up," when he takes one leap in the air, and in mid-air kicks out his armored leg with a violence that would do credit to a champion hurdler. The kick is intended to exorcize the evil spirit of death. That is the end of the program, which is repeated, *da capo, ad infin.*

The music for this dance is furnished by a couple of tom-toms, a flute, a hunting horn, and the singing of the youngsters, who attend the dance in large numbers. They clap their hands to the rhythm of the dancing and stamp their little feet as though they, too, were part of the ceremony. The great feature of the music, however, is the clanging of the bells on the armored legs, which is so perfect in time that one cannot detect a single misstep of a foot in this vast crowd of dancers. There were more than forty "star" dancers in the performance which I attended, and during the hour and a half that I watched them I looked for breaks in the rhythm, but I did not hear a bell that was out of time. The bells are like our sleighbells, and they are made of iron tied to strings of rawhide, five in a row. These rows begin at the ankle and run up to the joint of the hip and thigh at intervals of two or three inches. The harness is tremendously heavy and could not weigh an ounce under fifteen pounds. The fantastic headgear of monkey skins and cow tails, feathers and waving plumes, adds "local color" to the dance and helps to make the whole spectacle distinctively native.

THE WAKAMBA

LEAVING the Wanyika after a pleasant stay
of two weeks among them, we returned to
Mariakani station on the Uganda Railroad for
the bi-weekly train, and were pleasantly surprised to see the sparks from the wood-burning
engine splash around the toy locomotive.
There was the usual haggling and fighting
about the surplus amount of luggage to be
crowded into the little guard van. But a
freight train brought the balance, which we
had to leave on the platform, after only one
day's delay. We therefore moved on farther
west for a distance of some two hundred miles,
and feasted our eyes on the large herds of the
various kinds of antelope and deer which ran
a distance, then faced the train expectantly,
and again turned and ran another few hundred
yards to renew their caprices. Ostriches paced
a few hundred yards to the right, parallel to
the roadbed, moving their long legs in measured inverted V's and clapping their feather-

less wings like useless Cupid appendages. This sign of life at least gave us an intimation that at last we had left the effete coast and pierced into the real Africa of the hunter's dreams, with Ukamba as the gate.

I always had a great desire to know more about the Wakamba. In my earlier missionary days I used to watch them in camp. The joy at the killing of a zebra or kongoni and the relish with which they used to eat the raw or slightly roasted meat and tear away at it with their saw-like teeth had a fascination for me which made me always anxious to know them better. Hence it was with a pleasant anticipation that I swung off the train at Kapiti Plains and pitched camp on the very spot which ten years ago had sheltered our beloved and lamented Theodore Roosevelt.

To a certain extent I was disappointed, because they had changed so much since the early days of 1900, when they were still in their savage glory. They are now a mixed breed, and civilizing influences, although not entirely successful, have mitigated their raw savagery of old.

"Arizona all over again," said my companion when we struck Kapiti Plains and had left the Roosevelt camp. Nothing to be seen but a

slight bluff at the end of a gently sloping plain.
The bluff, however, had witnessed many a killing in former days, when the lions made Kapiti
the Eldorado of big game hunters and when
Stony Athi was THE lion cage of the world.
Kongoni were still to be found in great herds
and little did I know that I was prophesying
when I remarked to my companion what a
waste of good teeth this plain contained in the
many bleached skulls which the plain revealed
almost at every rod.

It happened to be the very ground where
the Wakamba get their teeth renewed from the
rich choice scattered along that road. It is
unbelievable that the Wakamba should be able
to insert these artificial teeth so skillfully that
they won't come out after they are screwed
into their place, but it is a fact notwithstanding that the Ukamba youth whose picture I
have both in still and moving photograph has
no less than six of these artificial teeth screwed
into his upper jaw. He took one of them out
before the camera and put it back again, and
if it were not for that exhibition I would have
joined the chorus of skeptics who have smiled
in my face when I related the phenomenon.

The Wakamba, or, as they call themselves,
Akamba, are a Bantu tribe occupying a large

territory which begins west of the station of
Mariakani on the Uganda Railroad and which
borders on the Wanyika lands to Athi Station
on the same line, at which point it converges
with the territory of the Wakikuyu. The population of the Wakamba territory is estimated
at 235,000, a figure based on the returns from
the hut taxes which the British government has
imposed on the Wakamba tribe. This population is scattered over an area of about 150
miles from east to west, and an irregular
stretch from north to south.

The tribe is essentially of Bantu stock, although the many raids which they have made
on the Wakikuyu and the Masai have brought
about an admixture of Nilotic and Hamitic
blood, for the slaves taken on these marauding
excursions have left their mark on their progeny. Except for this infusion of Nilotic and
Hamitic blood the Wakamba are a pure race,
for they are most exclusive when it comes to
taking in strangers by intermarriage.

Clan life is not highly developed in the
Wakamba tribe. According to the best available information, there are only eight original
clans, and some of these, like the Atui, are
subdivided into three clans which may not intermarry among themselves, although any

member of the three may marry a girl from the mother clan. This peculiar regulation necessarily tends toward a degree of inbreeding and seems to contradict a statement made by Mr. Hobley in his book on the Wakamba to the effect that they are probably the purest extant tribe of Bantu. I base this argument on the fact that the Wakamba are insensible to the deleterious effects of inbreeding, whereas the other tribes are keenly aware of them. Moreover, there are fewer totems among the Wakamba than there are among most of the other Bantu tribes. Several clans have the same totem, and as the totem is the chief distinguishing mark by which the purity of the clan is guarded and by which inbreeding is avoided, I come to the conclusion that the practices of the Wakamba unavoidably result in alliances by which close relatives become the parents of a less pure progeny.

The small list of totems also points to the same conclusion. Where many totems define the limits of mating selection with an ironclad barrier about the preserves, there is less danger of mistakes, so that this line of demarcation guards against subsequent degeneration. What I have said about the preservation of the purity of the tribe may be repeated in regard to the original prominence of the tribal perfection as a Bantu group. We must bear in mind that, after all, language is the strongest criterion or factor dividing the Nilotic and Bantu camps. The language of the Wakamba is not so purely Bantu as that, for example, of the Baganda or Urundi. This characteristic may be ascribed to the strong influence of the Masai strain in the tribe, but the fact remains that the limited and generic nature of the Wakamba totems contrasted with the long litany of these guardian angels of purity among other tribes seems to call for some other explanation of the "distinction" conferred on the Wakamba.

The Wakamba muster only four animal totems—the tortoise (the general totem of all the Wakamba), the pig, the bush buck, and the Mbungu bird. The other totems are certain parts of an animal, such as the liver, the head or the lungs of any, or, in some cases, a specified beast. This, I think, is not a great enough variety of interdicted food specifics to prevent inbreeding. However, I merely mention this matter to indicate that clan development among the Wakamba is not especially pronounced.

Wakamba huts are very unpretentious

abodes. They are built of twigs in the form of a beehive, circular and not more than fifteen feet in diameter. They are divided in two parts, one partition serving to permit a certain amount of privacy for the father and mother of the family. Parents and children have separate fireplaces.

Small as the huts are, there is a great deal of ceremony attached to the building of them. Like the Wanyika, the Wakamba are not gregarious and each family has its own village; therefore when one speaks of the building of a house, one means the establishment of a village, to which much superstition is attached.

On my way from Machakos to Stony Athi I saw an old man throwing stones from a central position which he had taken up, and when he turned from one quarter to another, throwing stones to the four directions of the wind, I thought he was performing some pagan rite or other and naturally wanted to know what it was all about. One of my guides maintained that he was picking a building site. Being more or less interested in real estate, I thought I might pick up some new information for my real estate agent friends, therefore I "stopped, looked and listened," and this is what it all meant.

The medicine man must select the site for the village, and he arrives at his choice by throwing stones in various directions. When he is satisfied that he has located the right place he sprinkles the area with the blood of a goat and with the contents of the goat's stomach. The prospective builder offers up this goat, but he does not eat it, for the meat is the *baccici* (fee) for the medicine man.

The *boma* (enclosure) is built first, and on its completion the family sleeps four days in the open *boma* under a scanty shelter. It is required that husband and wife cohabit there on the second and fourth nights, lest there be no more children. When all of these rites have been performed correctly, poles for the building of the house are brought from the forest or the woods. When the poles are planted, a little grass is spread over them and a meal of porridge is cooked. A portion of this food is smeared on the poles; the family partakes of the meal; and the rest of it, divided into four pieces, is strewn on the floor, along with six pieces of meat, if meat is part of the meal. On the second night of their residence in this framework the parents must again perform their marital obligations lest ill fortune strike the house. When finally the house is erected, the owner must prepare a feast for his relatives and slaughter two goats to initiate the building properly. Later on a second and possibly a third house may be added, along with small grain huts.

The Wakamba are now an agricultural and pastoral tribe by occupation, and they derive their foodstuffs from their labors, although originally they were purely pastoral. At present they live principally on grains, especially maize, mtama, mawele and wimbi, which they fuse into a porridge which they like to mix with honey or milk. Green bananas and Indian corn are their choicest delicacies. They retain a special relish for a dish which they used to regard as a staple when they hunted and herded the cattle which is now too valuable to eat. This entrée is the raw blood of an animal—either deer or bullock—which they extract from the jugular vein. The animal need not be killed to provide this "pièce de résistance," for the blood can be tapped without slaughter. The liquid is churned in a gourd and drunk from small leaves, which take the place of spoons.

To obtain the blood of the bullock, they throw the animal on the ground and tighten a rope of rawhide about its neck to accumulate the blood. Then they shoot an arrow into the jugular vein, from which the blood forthwith spurts in great quantities. Sometimes they apply their lips directly to the wound to quench their thirst for their favorite non-intoxicating beverage. As soon as the rope is removed from the bullock's neck the bleeding stops and the animal jumps up and bolts away, none the worse for the experience.

The Wakamba maintain a gruesome system of tribal marks, which seems to be dying out, although many of the younger members of the tribe still indulge in it. The older generations have obeyed the code religiously and take pride in it, and they condemn the youths for not carrying on the tradition. The chief custom is to chip the teeth, and there are special artists who perform this ceremony. They use a small chisel and hammer with which they knock off minute pieces of the four incisors and sometimes the eye teeth, until the teeth look like spikes. The upper jaw consequently resembles a fine saw. The artist chisels around the nerve without striking it, taking off the enamel but leaving the cement protection for the root. A minimum of enamel is left so as not to endanger the cement. The result of the operation is that certain teeth are made ex-

BLOOD DRINKING OF THE WAKAMBA
In the time of famine the Wakamba do not kill their animals
but extract and drink their blood.
Preparing for the operation. Shooting the arrow into the bull's neck
to extract the blood. The bull is bled from the jugular vein
in the neck.
Drinking the warm, raw, foaming blood with spoons made from the
leaves of a tree.

TYPES AND CUSTOMS

Wakamba types

Ukamba milk maid

Funnell hats of the Wakamba

ceedingly sharp for the purpose of eating raw meat and its shred fibers. The juicy substance of the meat is thereby extracted with ease and the natives derive the full benefit of their food.

These dental manipulations give the Wakamba an unpleasant appearance, for the best feature of the negro is the healthy and regular line of teeth which is naturally his. When the teeth are damaged the surrounding features seem the uglier for it. The Wakamba aggravate matters by breaking out the two central incisors of the lower jaw in order to ward off starvation during an attack of tetanus. The Wakamba seem to revel in sacrificing health for beauty—and for fancy. As a result of these dental mutilations the condition of their gums and mouths in general is deplorable. Festering sets in almost universally and pus forms about the roots of the teeth, generally causing the loss of the teeth. Pyorrhea is common, and more serious mouth infections occur frequently. Yet there is a compensation for these evils, because the Wakamba have developed some remarkable dentists.. Lost upper teeth are replaced with new ones obtained from the kongoni or hartebeest. These artificial teeth are grafted on the cavities and hammered in until they remain in place. The new teeth are filed or chipped to resemble the original set. We saw one young Mukamba who had six teeth extracted and replaced in this manner, and he was able to take them all out and screw them in again for eating purposes. Yet despite the startling dental accomplishments of the Wakamba I found that most of the natives have their mouths in a shocking condition.

What the Wakamba lack orally they seem to gain in sight and hearing. These senses are developed abnormally. The Wakamba can see a long distance and can describe an animal accurately when we can scarcely see the beast. This ability gives one an uncanny feeling. Their auricular sense is equally amazing. They can speak to one another in ordinary conversational tones at a distance of one hundred yards without difficulty.

What makes the Wakamba such fine trackers and gunbearers is this abnormal sense of hearing. This sense is so acutely developed that a white man in pursuit would have no chance with them. Their sense of auricular perception is as phenomenal as the sense of odor in an elephant.

Another tribal mark which is very common is one which seems to be equally common in

the United States. It is the method of beauty
culture which compels the women to pick out
their eyebrows. Some of the natives (the
Wakamba, of course!) go so far as to carry
a pair or more of tweezers with them wherever
they travel. The operation, I suppose, is painful, but beauty will not be gainsaid and the
natives will sacrifice nothing more willingly
than their eyebrows. Considering the black-
ness of the Africans, the absence of eyebrows
really makes little difference, for the beauty
spots are of the same color as the rest of the
skin and the hair; but the natives seem to find
an æsthetic delight in the operation—and with
the women, that is ample ground for anything!

Another and more cruel mark is the scarification of their skins, especially on the abdomen and the breasts. This habit, together with
the fashion of wearing copper and brass rings
and waistbands, causes an almost universal
complaint of skin trouble. There are few
women in the Wakamba district who are not
afflicted with coarse and often diseased skins.
Their condition is aggravated by their insist-
ence on greasing themselves with a crude mixture of rancid butter. This combination of
irritants will leave little occasion for a medical
rechercheur to look further for the origin and

causes of the prevalent dermal trouble. The fact that the natives wear tanned and cured goatskins, which are seldom if ever cleaned or washed, does not help to cure the disease, for the apparel absorbs a great part of the matter given off by the body and retains the putrefied excretions of the sores.

To cicatrize these marks on the skin in various patterns they use a knife and a needle simultaneously, yet not a sigh escapes these brave maidens when they submit in the cause of beauty.

The ear also cannot escape the ravages of mutilation which are demanded by the implacable law of fashion. Our own earrings hang easily from the tiniest puncture, but the Wakamba affect chains of enormous weight and dimensions, and the thousand and one other articles which they carry in their ears could not be accommodated unless the whole lobe of the ear were split open and extended. Even this generous measure does not fill the Wakamba beauty's cup of joy. She must carry her ornaments not only at the bottom of the ear but at the top. So she makes a clean job of it—and the result is an ear that looks as though it were knotted and folded over with the weight of the trinkets.

Nor is the scalp immune from beautifying artifices. The scalp is treated with relative tenderness, but the results are divers and bewildering. It would be futile to attempt to catalogue the many patterns in which the hair is shaved. Moons, half-moons, quarter crescents and stars are very popular; twists, spirals, prisms—all the figures known to mathematics and trigonometry are found on the fashion plates in the tonsorial department of the Wakamba. To leave two or more tufts growing after the bulk of the hair has been removed is the height of good form. Sometimes one sees a beautiful pyramid standing straight up on the top of the head to lend enchantment to Uka's dome. The whims of Lady Fashion are strange and elusive—but so long as her devotees are ready to pay the price in blood and pain, what may a man say in protest?

Closely allied to the tribal marks is the question of dress—another concession to vanity. The men are indifferent in the matter, for their personal pride is not developed in this direction. They seem to be almost callous to self-respect and are content to let a blanket cover their nakedness. Before the advent of blankets they wore skins, and they were not particular whether the skins protected them above or below the waist. A portable chair and a snuff-box—ah, that were happiness enow for them! But the women! Well, "you know what women are." There was a banquet in Nairobi at which most of the diners were in what is known as "full" evening costume. A facetious old-timer in British East Africa remarked that the more clothes the African women adopted, the less the white women seemed to wear. I shall not pass judgment on this uncharitable observation, but it brings out the point that the African women are not so insensible to clothes as they used to be.

However, the Wakamba women are an exception, for they always had an interest in dress and they have a prescribed wear for each stage of life through which they pass. They begin their career with a little beaded life-belt to which other beaded coils are added until, at the age of ten or twelve, they have accumulated quite a wide band of strings of beads. This band, in most cases, is wider than a cholera belt, and it comes in every conceivable color. At this age they begin to indulge in jewelry, such as armlets, necklets, arm and elbow coils of brass and copper, and all the rest of the feminine gewgaws. They pile on neck rings until they are burdened with a sizeable stock of hardware, although, as I have mentioned, these ornaments produce scars and irritations on the skin. The girls always wear a little apron, but when they are about ten years old they put on well-cured skins or a cloth mantle thoroughly soaked in castor oil and lava dust. This garment is supposed to last a lifetime, and as they advance in age the women may add a blanket or two under the cloth. The old women wear a skin, over or under which they frequently wrap a cloth mantle. In their old age they retain whatever luxury life has provided for them.

Marriage customs are, of course, absorbingly interesting always and everywhere, and I never pass a tribe without investigating into its ceremonial customs and methods of bridal acquisition. This, to my way of thinking, and the dance give one a better key to the status of culture in a given tribe than any other usage displayed. I like the old Baganda system the best, because there they use every method known in the matrimonial mill. I wrote a thesis on that question, and I believe that the system of matrimony reflects the mental attitude of a clan or tribe, in regard to the moral status, very accurately. It is for this reason particularly that I look upon the Wakamba as an unmoral people, having no regard for their bargains once a contract is made.

Marriage is a ceremony about which the Wakamba trouble themselves even less than the Wanyika; with them, it will be remembered, marriage is purely a matter of commerce. Not that the Wakamba overlook the important part of the transaction which means so many cows or goats added to the herds of the bride's father, but there is even less ceremony in the giving of the daughter and her departure from home than there is with the Wanyika. With the Wakamba, marriage is a deal in which the young man is fleeced.

The young man and the young woman become acquainted, and when there is a mutual understanding the prospective bridegroom informs his father who, accompanied by a couple of goats, calls on the young woman's father. The goats are handed over to the father-in-law-to-be, and after the import of the call is explained the two men confer about the prospects of their children and the young man's father departs. Three days later he returns with three she-goats and another conference takes place. Seven days later he pays another visit, bringing with him six goats. A subsequent call enriches the girl's father by twenty to forty additional goats—and then the recipient recalls that he has neglected to demand one or two bulls. When the final animal offering is delivered, along with three or four gourds of "Tembo," the fathers drink to the bargain. While the conviviality is at its height, the girl's family is informed of the transaction, and this is a cue for the men to prepare for a battle.

Six brothers or other relatives of the groom leave their homes well armed, and approach the house of the girl. She, knowing the day and the hour, strolls into the field where her brothers are herding the flocks. The six stalwarts attempt to carry her off. The brothers contest the maneuver. If the kidnapers are repulsed, the bridegroom is obliged to forfeit ten additional goats. The whole procedure is not unlike the forcible bride-snatching of the early Teutons.

The girl, having been kidnaped successfully, is taken to the hut of her father-in-law, where she is treated with the utmost consideration, and after the birth of the first child the husband builds his own hut and forms his own establishment. Three weeks after this event the bride's mother receives fourteen bunches of bananas, one male sheep, one large male goat and other food. Then the young man halves a young bullock, one half of which goes to the mother-in-law.   When he has delivered this present he suggests to his wife that she go with him out of the village of her parents.   He looks about as though he were suspicious of trickery, and when he reaches the village limits he takes the girl by the hand and they go home to stay. Hereafter the young husband never speaks to his mother-in-law again, and he must avoid her should they meet on the road.

The day after this ceremony three of the girl's female friends go to the hut of the young couple and receive some beads.   Here they stay for three days, during which time they weep and lament the departure of their old companion.

Sometimes an elopement takes place, but if the girl's father objects, the girl must be returned and there must be a wedding according to custom.   It is quite common for the Wakamba to lend their wives to visiting brothers or clansmen, and there is no resentment on the part of the lady who receives this change of venue without being consulted.

The Wakamba are exogamous in their choice of life partners, except where there is a subdivision of the clan, in which case, as I have pointed out before, there may be an endogamous union.

Birth customs among the Wakamba are very peculiar. The mother is confined standing up, clinging to a horizontal pole, with her limbs spread out wide to facilitate the birth. There are two women in attendance, one to receive the baby and the other to sever the umbilical cord, which she immediately buries close to the house. The mother may not leave the hut for twenty days after the birth, and she is fed by the women in attendance. At the end of this period the parents have their first ceremonial cohabitation, during which the child is placed on the breast of the mother to make certain the birth of other children. This continues until the first menstruation occurs, after which the mother carries the child on her shoulder. When a child is born feet foremost, it is a bad omen, and such children are circumcised apart from the rest and are always looked at askance. They can never find anyone willing to marry them and practically become outcasts.

Formerly it was the custom to bury alive a girl born as one of twins, because she was thought to bring ill fortune to the family.

Beer is brewed on the day of the birth, to be consumed three days later at a feast given by the father, who also kills a goat or a bullock, depending on his wealth. Six months before the expected birth of a child the woman ceases to live with her husband. During the full term of carrying the child, she must not eat butter, for butter is supposed to kill the child. (Unmarried women who have conceived consume butter as an abortive measure.) Nor must the mother eat honey during her pregnancy, because honey is fattening and would fatten the child to such an extent that the mother would die in giving birth or become incapable of delivering it.

The Wakamba have little respect for the dead, and for the rank and file of the people there is not even a burial. Peasants and women are thrown out into the bush without being placed under the ground, and their bodies are allowed to rot or to be eaten by the jackals and the hyenas. Usually the beasts of prey deliver the last rites in their own ghastly manner. The common dead are even stripped of their clothing, if they have any, and they are neither mourned nor honored with a cortège when they are disposed of in the bush.

I had no opportunity to observe the funeral rites of the Wakamba, but I am told that their system is a heartless one. Battlefield hyenas of the Napoleonic wars have much in common with these gentry. The chiefs and heads of villages fare a little better, but there is none of the elaborate mourning which is common in other tribes. The natives dig a grave for a prominent man and deposit his naked body in the aperture. The spirit is fed from time to time by food which is left on the plot where he is laid away. No cultivation is permitted on this land, and soon it is overgrown with weeds, which generally are the mark of the resting place of a chief.

There is a prescribed mourning term of twenty days to be observed by the relatives of the departed, but this is in reality a period of feasting rather than a time of sorrow. Great quantities of beer are consumed, and there are dances, but not the kind of dances which the Wanyika perform as a religious observance. The village mourns one day for a chief, and there is a continuous wailing from morning until night. The wife, the children and the brothers do not shave their hair for seven days. All marital rights are suspended for two days after a death, however humble, for it is believed that a child conceived under such circumstances is shadowed by death, and that even if it survived it would be the slave of lethal spirits. Nor is there eating for one day after a death, lest the gaunt spirit share the feast and reap more victims. There is wailing for three hours after every death, not for sorrow but to expel the evil spirit from the community.

Being a graduate in Jurisprudence with a hobby for ancient Anglo-American legal institutions, I revel in old, "moyen age" and modern jury methods and our ancestral ordeals by water and fire, which together with our other systems might almost have been taken "en bloc" into the Wakamba procedure. Of course, they have no plowshares nor pitch, but otherwise they follow us pretty closely. The "Kithito" particularly is a remarkable institution.

The Wakamba have some odd methods for meting out justice. They favor various forms of ordeals which are similar to the early English system of trying a case. One instance is ordeal by fire. The medicine man heats an iron, confers a certain power on the heated iron and thereafter hands it to the accused, who, he says, shall not be burned if he is not guilty. If, however, the iron hurts him, his guilt is mani-

COURT OF JUSTICE OF THE WAKAMBA
The convicted culprit is ordered to be flogged.

SCARIFICATIONS
A close view of the scarifications of an ordinary design of a
Wakamba woman.

fest. There is also a water test, which is employed when several persons are suspected of a given misdeed and when there is no specific evidence against any one of them. The suspects are placed in a semicircle by the medicine man, who, after lining up the persons on trial, fills a gourd with water and begins to revolve it. If the guilty one is in the party the gourd will spout forth water when it is turned toward this individual, whose guilt is thereupon declared.

Something approximating the sanctity of our oath is administered in a case where there is no direct evidence, but where strong suspicion attaches to a certain individual. The suspect is brought before the "Nzama," or native council of elders, who sit in judgment. The accused is asked over and over again whether he is guilty of the offense with which he is charged. If he declines to answer satisfactorily he is finally confronted with the "Kithito," or sacred horn, before which he must swear his innocence. The sacred horn, which is one of a kongoni or hartebeest, or of a bullock, is filled with weeds and a certain poison. The "Kithito" is placed on the rocks and a little twig is laid on the sacred emblem. Thereupon the accused is charged by the medicine man to demonstrate his innocence on the holy fetish, and he is informed that if he swears falsely he is bound to die; if he swears truly, the stain will be removed from his character.

So strongly do the natives believe in the efficacy of the oath that if they are guilty they will refuse to swear on the "Kithito" and confess their crime rather than face certain death. If they are innocent, they make their oath without fear. The "Kithito" is much in use at the present time, and it is the best friend of the officers of the courts among the Wakamba, because it weeds out many cases which otherwise would have to be tried in regular courts.

The chief or any elder may administer the oath, and if a quorum be lacking, any of the natives may sit in judgment. The form of the oath is to take up the twig from the horn and to hold it out to the judges, who are thereby convinced of the innocence of the defendant. Sometimes the twig remains on the horn, and the oath-taker receives a similar twig with which to touch the other. The "Kithito" is used also to make peace between two clans of the Wakamba, and it is handed down from father to son, becoming a traditional sacred relic in the family. The different foods and medicines with which the horn is filled are renewed on occasion, and when the "Kithito" is to be used it is smeared with the fat of a sheep.

Capital punishment is not known among the Wakamba, but a code which sounds like the early "dooms" of the English courts is used by the elders and the medicine men. For instance, an assault whereby the head of the complainant is severely injured is atoned for by one goat or ox, or even by as much as five cows, if the hurt is disfiguring. Rape is punished by a forfeit of two goats—three, if the girl has conceived. In this crime the girl receives the skin and the elders consume the meat.

When a person proves to be a habitual thief or a constant nuisance, he is "removed from the face of the earth," but not by capital punishment. He (or she) is warned repeatedly that he will be reported to the heads of his family or clan and that thereafter the clan will be held responsible for his actions. If, after such warning, there is no improvement in his behavior, the family or clan is looked upon as a menace to public safety and dealt with accordingly. As a result of this law the clan usually gives its delinquent member another warning; if this ultimatum is ignored a certain member

of the family is detailed to kill the offender—
and this duty is generally performed with
alacrity.

Succession rights are equitable among the
tribe. When the head of a family dies his
wives are inherited by his brothers, who appor-
tion them among themselves, and the property
passes on to the sons. Daughters are not
"named in the will," but their uncles are morally bound to support them.

Having had such a good time at the
Wanyika dance, I was much disappointed in
that of the Wakamba. There seemed to be a
lack of æsthetic or mystical meaning to it, or
if there was any I could not find it, except the
diabolical meaning of the witch dance.

Unlike the Wanyika, the Wakamba have
very poor dances. They compensate for the
lack of quality in the dancing by holding these
functions as frequently as possible; there are
terpsichorean sessions daily, whenever a sufficient number of dancers can be gathered together. A semicircle is formed, with men at
the lower end of the line and the women on the
other. The men beat a drum, which they hold
between themselves and the women, and they
continue raising the sound throughout the evolutions. The partners assume a "cheek-to-

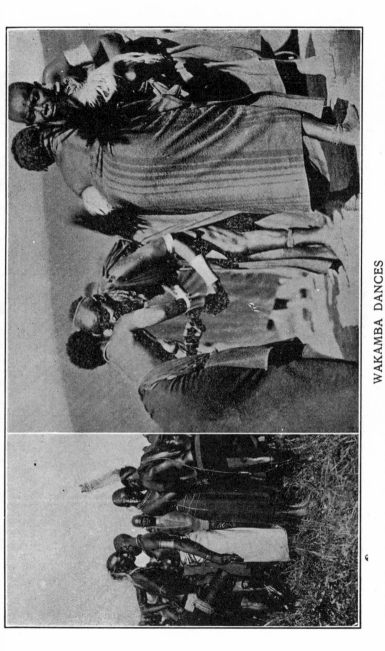

WAKAMBA DANCES

Wakamba cheek dance of the younger set.

Wakamba witch dance of the elder women keeps evil designing men at bay.

RACIAL DIFFERENCES IN AFRICAN TRIBES

An Ethnological observation made by Dr. Vanden Bergh. From Lake Albert Nyanza into the interior the tribes grow smaller. Dr. Vanden Bergh selected a specimen of each and photographed them together to show their racial differences. The tallest is the Alour, six feet and more next Wolordy average five feet to five feet three inches, next Wanyari

cheek" posture—as though they were in one of our fashionable grillrooms—but only the men move their feet. The women remain still below the waist, but they wriggle the upper parts of their bodies in a manner that reminds one of the "shimmy," while their arms hang limply at their sides. The men and women come together at the start of the dance proper—or improper, if you prefer—and stay in one place throughout. A shrill whistle accompanies the dance, which, however, cannot be said to possess artistic or rhythmic elements.

The old women have a witch dance which is rather eery in its effect. The movements are similar to those indulged in by the younger dancers except that the old women do not indulge in the voluptuous contortions of their younger sisters. There is something sensual in the antics of the half-naked young women, but the old women behave in harmless fashion. The sight is rather disgusting on account of the ugly appearance of the old creatures. If the dance had a pleasant connotation no one could cavil at the old women having their meed of pleasure, but the witch dance carries with it a dreadful meaning. This dance is not only intended for a possible future execution of the kind that I have described (the death sentence of a habitual thief or other malefactor), but where such a death is impending the old women who have a grievance against the victim dance this witch dance to implore the spirit of death to come and seize the object of their hatred. Formerly it was not uncommon to execute an old woman past usefulness or any woman who no longer could bear children or perform the ordinary drudge of labor.

When such an execution were foreseen other aged women would gather and hold the witch dance partly for self-protection and partly to invoke the vengeance of the spirits of the ancestors on the guilty parties who intended to kill the aged woman.

There is little to be said of the industries of the Wakamba. Although the men are not quite so listless and lackadaisical as the Wanyika, there is little energy to be found. The men occasionally assist the women in the fields, but they are very unreliable workers. The only labor at which they do not lack enterprise is the making of beer, of which they are abnormally fond. It is not easy at this time to see them at this task, for brewing has been prohibited by the government on account of the excessive drinking and the consequent lawlessness.

The worst feature I remembered of them
from the old days was their boisterous and dangerous condition when they had indulged in
their "tembo," an alcoholic inebriant made of
sugarcane and much worse than any found on
the old caravan route. Although I had little
experience with the Wakamba, I do remember plastering some nasty gashes which were
the results of overindulgence.

The Wakamba are notorious for their passion for drink, and they cannot get enough of
their own sugar beer, the manufacture of which
I shall discuss later. For the consumption of
this native drink they have an especial location
which they call the "Thomi." This reservation
is an open space in front of the village, and
it is swept religiously every morning by the
young boys of the village. The sanctity of the
"rendez-vous" is so stringent that all visitors
are barred. It is a sort of exclusive club for
old men, and should a woman happen to stray
into this bacchic shrine she would be beaten and
driven out like an intrusive dog. Here the
men drink and play their games and pass the
best part of the day. A fire is built in the center, where the wise old heads may sit about and
discourse on the topics of the times.

Another intoxicant, or more correctly, soporific, is snuff. Every Mukamba carries a snuff-box, which is his principal article of accouter-ment. The natives are very proud of these containers, and they have some very attractive boxes in the shape of a small ball of hollow wood with an ivory cover. The snuff mer-chants are the chief attraction of the native market, where they squat in little groups of six to ten. The snuff mart is the center of keenest haggling in the trading place, and if you have ever relished snuff or have become a slave to it, get some Ukamba snuff, and I guarantee you that it will be the last you'll whiff. I bought some to please them, and my nose still retains the memory of the ven-ture.

The British government, always anxious to put down native abuses and yet desirous to preserve the ancient traditions, has modified the drinking bouts in a most diplomatic man-ner. There are certain ceremonies for which the native beer is prescribed, such as births, circumcisions, espousals, thanksgivings for the crops, sick healings and sacrifice festivals. For these rites a certain quantity of beer is "sine qua non," and the government issues permits for its use only when these solemnities occur. The natives therefore feel that the officials are not interfering with their traditions, but at the same time the consumption of sugar beer is diminished. They used to make their beer from sugarcane, and later from raw sugar. Both commodities were placed under an embargo, and now they import molasses, which was not included in the statute. However, molasses is soon to share the fate of its predecessors.

The manner in which this sugar beer is made from the raw material is rather ingenious. Owing to the native resourcefulness there is little more required than the sugarcane, a grater, such as the nutmeg grater, and a piece of string. The cane, stripped of its bark, is grated and produces a sort of shredded pulp. The pulp is then shaped into a loaf and wound around with the string to make it cohere. When the loaf has been reasonably packed it is wrung like a piece of clothing in the wash. The juice is the beer, which is ready to be consumed after one day of fermenting. To facilitate the operation the natives dip the fiber in water, which also tends to dilute the beer.

There are, of course, a number of artisans who perform various tasks like blacksmithing, carpentry, and chairmaking. Blacksmithing is a profession which passes from father to son.

The other trades are adopted by voluntary application. The scarifier has the dual distinction of being artist and medicine man, and his profession is one much sought for because every Makamba is anxious to be tattooed in the best possible style. To perform this operation perfectly, three instruments are needed: a piece of charcoal, a sharp knife, and a hook resembling our button-hook. The charcoal traces the lines along which the scarifying is to be done; the knife makes ever so slight an incision and the hook turns over one side of the skin so that the tattoo will grow out in the correct manner.

The chainmaker has an equally limited set of tools. He carries a pair of pliers, a steel needle which looks like our knitting needles, and a small flat stone or board on which to roll his long string of links. The dexterity of this man is marvelous. He makes a string of links in an instant and he cuts and puts them together while you wait.

The ring maker is not so great an expert although his science demands that he leave the muscles, arteries and veins of the arms and legs sufficiently free so that there is no atrophying or impediment in the natural flow of the blood. He must take

WAKAMBA DENTISTRY
The Wakamba chip their teeth for the eating of raw meat. It is
also a mark of beauty and brutal distinction.
The dentist at work.
The completed job.   Raw meat eating.

ENLARGED NAVALS ARE THE RESULT OF POOR CONFINEMENT

care that the rings about an armored leg do not press against the flesh. Many a woman is seen with a swollen arm where the winding of the thick wire has obstructed the easy and natural flow of blood through her veins and arteries. A woman who entrusts herself to an inefficient coiler has to suffer the consequences of his awkwardness as well as the pangs imposed by her vanity.

The chipping process involved in the tribal teeth marking which I have outlined is work requiring considerable nicety of execution. The dentist's paraphernalia look like a carpenter's outfit. The chisel with which he chips the enamel is about two inches long and one inch wide and not very sharp. He lays the boy on whom he is operating on his lap so that the head rests on the thigh, with subsidiary support from the abdomen. He places the chisel on the patient's teeth and hammers away at it gently with a light stick. This operation continues for hours on end and it is repeated day after day until the teeth have acquired the orthodox tribal shape. Their sawlike teeth as I said before always had me wondering in the olden days and now I had the opportunity, I went into this phase of Wakamba barbarism very particularly; and the results were some startling features and some wonderful pictures.

Stoolmaking is another artistic profession. The stool has the form of the familiar milking chair. Three round legs are inserted through half the full diameter. Some of the chairs have a copper or brass band turned around the edge, and a brass or copper inlay on the surface. The copper wire is placed in a little groove in the hard wood of which the chair is constructed.

There are endless ornaments made of beads, including necklets, armlets and bracelets. Patterns artistic and not so artistic, are to be found in profusion; both the men and women produce these articles—all except the intimate bead apron which the women wear. This bit of Wakamba lingerie is made only by women. The beaded ornaments are woven so finely that American women would be proud to possess bags made by the natives.

The natives also make fiber bags, which the women carry suspended from their heads by a strap. The fiber for these receptacles is stripped from the bark of young saplings of a certain tree and chewed by the women, whose sharp teeth are most useful in cutting the bark into a thread-like fiber. Wherever the teeth have punctured the bark, a strip of fiber is loosened so that it may be detached. The fiber is then twisted into a string and woven into the desired form.

Honey making also may be classified as a Wakamba industry. The beehives are hung high in the air. They are wooden cylinders, four feet long with a diameter of a foot and a half. They look more like idols or like food stores for the spirits than like beehives, but I am told that they produce the sweetest honey to be found in British East Africa. The hives are not unlike the native drums, and sometimes these cylinders serve both as a source of nourishment and as a musical instrument.

For hunting the natives use the bow and arrow. Their arrows are the deadliest known, on account of the potent poisons with which they are tipped. Poisoned arrows, however, are more common in warfare than in hunting. The poison is prepared from the sap of the Murai tree and the fangs of the scorpion. When not in use, they are wrapped in a thin covering of skin or fiber which comes loose when the arrow is shot. The natives are sure shots at a distance of one hundred feet. Another weapon which sometimes comes into play is a double edged sword about two feet long.

They also have a wired hunting club which is said to do great damage both in battle and in the hunt.

The only lasting impression that I took away from the Wakamba was that recorded in my nostrils—and it was not a pleasant impression. To protect their skins from cracking in the great heat, the natives daub their bodies with rancid butter, the odor of which is beyond the vocabulary of polite description. And in case of malaria or other disease, it is well to keep the natives away from the camp with an armed guard, if necessary, or they will augment the nausea, though they be as much as forty yards away.

THE WAKIKUYU

IF I were forced to make a selection of location where to spend the balance of my days on the African continent I would without hesitation plant myself in Kikuyu within easy reach of Nairobi. There is some indefinable atmosphere of freshness about Kikuyu which puzzles one for an assignment of cause. Is it the mild almost semi-tropical climate, the purity of the air, the evergreen aspect of the country, the deliciousness of the all year round fruit, the green velvet fields, the perennial soft murmurs of the crystal clear brooks or the gentle manners of the natives, or probably, the combination of all these attractive attributes? Be this as it may of the many times I have visited Kikuyu there is only one universal memory impressed on my mind and that is a spirit of calmness, resignation and easy abandonment which makes the leisure of a vacation so absorbingly desirable. All these influences are to be found in Kikuyu. If my memory does not fail me I think the average elevation of that district is a little above 4,000 feet.

I cannot recall a sweltering hot day nor a chilly spell which one finds, for instance, a little farther west on the Mao plateau. No violent storms like in Kavirondo or Uganda are encountered here. I believe the natives of Kikuyu have a tradition which claims that the great Mungu waited to watch the effect of all his other domains he had created and then gathered all the choicest qualifications of the different parts of the earth and bestowed them on the region of Kikuyu to make it a garden paradise.

To emphasize the spirit of the district I would add that the people inhabiting that country do not manifest the extremes of lassitude nor the violence which one meets in almost every other tribe. It is remarkable to listen to their quiet contemplations uttered in their gentle singing drawl, and one marvels at the logical, clear-sighted deductions expounded in the ordinary course of conversation. I often sat listening to them when Father Caisack, their old white friend and father, drew them out. One such conversation still stands out in my memory, one in which the topic of the war was discussed. Evidently they had heard the news of the war from a French viewpoint with ample embellishments of atrocities committed. Without any animosity and with precise exactness I was asked as the latest arrival from Europe why the Allies had not made a clean sweep of such human monsters as the Germans were or marched on Berlin to execute the inevitable law of nature which we know as "an eye for an eye and a tooth for a tooth." The only answer I could think of was that reports in Kikuyu must have been slightly exaggerated. They evidently had compared warfare in Europe with the kind they knew between themselves and the Masai in which no quarter was given nor mercy expected. It came all the more as a shock to me because they are otherwise such a mild charactered people.

I have often thought that the environment of mild elements must have borne a great influence on their psychic formation and that their philosophic speculations are merely the result of an even temperament, caused by the suave topographic, geological and atmospheric circumstances, with which they are surrounded.

Measured in physical distance there was only a difference of about fifty miles between the central settlement of the wild Wakamba at Machakos and Nairobi, the pivot of the Kikuyu tribe, but the difference of the two peoples mentally, ethically and of instinct is almost infinite. This difference probably fastened itself on to me with more emphasis, because, this time I made the trip from Machakos to Nairobi by automobile, and was as it were, transplanted from the midst of one tribe into the heart of another in less than five hours.

In a word the Wakikuyu were always a conundrum to me. Their gentle manners, their harmonious tone of conversation, their unperturbed attitude, softened by a pleasing smile and languid pose attracted me.

Hence I had made up my mind to study them this time from a closer angle and resolved to get to the bottom of this conundrum if possible. Arriving in Nairobi I immediately inquired for my old friend and former companion of many a stroll through Kikuyu, the Rev. Father Caisack. I found that he had moved away from Nairobi and was living up country to get away from the host of new-fangled social creeds of the universe as seen from the Nairobi narrow vision of it, and devote his time and great talent to the "Kyuks" where indeed he has demonstrated his ability beyond question of a doubt. Then in the seclusion of the Mangu Mission I saw the Kyuks through the redeeming eyes of the old and beloved guide.

The most outstanding feature among the Wakikuyu which impresses one immediately on setting foot on Kikuyu soil is a custom which we might regard as the most horrible and inhuman practice in the world, were it not for the gentle nature and the kindly manners of the natives. These traits may be said to offset the apparently hard-hearted fashion in which they disposed of their dead.

On my way to the Mangu Mission I was far in the lead and alone when, stepping aside from the road, I stumbled on a human skull hidden in the grass. I picked it up and found that it bore all the evidences of having been recently stripped and picked. On my arrival at the mission I asked my old friend, the Reverend J. Caisack, an old French missionary, whether he had many experiences such as I had encountered that afternoon. The story that he told me was almost unbelievably gruesome.

It appears that the Wakikuyu never bury their dead, but throw their bodies out in the bush or high grass while the sufferer is still living. When the sick begin to show signs of the approaching end the relatives carry the dying person out from the hut and deposit him near the enclosure. When death has relieved the misery of the patient, the body left in the open soon begins to decompose. The odor attracts the hyenas toward the place where the body lies and these body snatchers take the funeral off the hands of the bereaved family. The custom sounds ghastly, yet when one understands the underlying reason for it, it seems less horrible.

The Wakikuyu are essentially a very religious, and pensive people with a philosophy which one would not expect to find in the wilds of the Kikuyu range. The mainspring and the principle of this creed is that sin is the root of all evil and that the result of sin is death. They further argue that death is contagious and that therefore no one must touch the dead for fear of being contaminated by the germ of death. Hence before a person dies he is carried out where no one needs to touch his body after the departure of the spirit. When a person dies suddenly the body is left in the hut and a hole is made in the wall so that the hyena will enter and drag the body out.

The consequences of these practices are more fanciful than the keenest imagination could encompass. Men who have recently lost their

GRUESOME METHOD IN WAKIKUYU OF DISPOSING OF THE DYING MEMBERS.
At nightfall the friends withdraw leaving the patient to the mercy of the hyenas.

TEMPLES OF WORSHIP
Sacred tree of Wakikuyu used in public worship
Construction of native Mission Church

mothers lie awake at night in their grief and
hear the dreaded brutes enter and carry away
the remains; and often they hear the crunching
of bones as the intruder tears the body apart.
A mother who has just lost her child lies groaning on her couch, distraught with the loss of
the only thing she loves in this world, and while
she is in the throes of her great sorrow she
hears the howling of the night prowler in the
distance, with its harrowing bark, coming
nearer and nearer until finally the infant's
body is slung over the neck of the beast and
carried away to be consumed by the scavenger
of the jungle. But so great is the religious
conviction of the natives that no attempt ever
is made to interfere with the feast of the wild
ogres and they are allowed to go unpunished
on their unholy and gruesome quest.

This feeling is so strong with the Wakikuyu
that even the dying themselves not only regard
the disposal of their bodies philosophically, but
even remind the bystanders and relatives that
the time has come for them to be carried away
because they feel death approaching. Instances are known where fathers of families
were heard to command their children to take
them out of the hut for fear that the contagion

of death might attack their progeny and the family die out through misguided filial affection and respect.

The Wakikuyu seem to be a race of philosophers with the stoical convictions so strongly impressed on their minds that no sacrifices are too great to satisfy the demands of their reasoning. The Spartans of old were not more insensible to pain and suffering nor to the ultimate test of courage (death) than the Wakikuyu who on first acquaintance would impress one as mere savages of a low order. It is only on further study of the race that one begins to appreciate their loyalty to their convictions which, extravagant and needlessly cruel as they may appear, are nevertheless an expression of a mental attitude which must be respected as we would have our own convictions honored.

Their tradition is that death is not a natural event but merely an accident brought about by the mistakes and transgressions of the persons responsible for the welfare of their dependents. It is not looked upon as a punishment but rather as a logical though avoidable result consequent on errors of judgment or action. Once the person has died, there is supposed to be a certain contagion which attaches to others

—mostly members of the family. The consequent series of deaths may come quickly or at length but they are certain to follow. Touching the body of a dead person is certain to kill the unfortunate one who has the temerity to lay his hand on the corpse. This helps to explain the seemingly cruel custom of carrying out the fatally ill before their death.

The teachings implied in this strange philosophy form a moral code which is also as inconsistent as the theory of death. For instance, there is no sin in anything that is according to the course of nature; conversely, all things contrary to nature are wicked. Accordingly fornication is no evil, nor is adultery, but incest, sodomy and similar crimes are so sinful that death will follow as a matter of course. After circumcision, girls and their lovers may live together without soiling their souls and even conception is not a thing of which they need be ashamed. Yet when the young man has made arrangements for marriage the girl looks upon him as her master, and will take another lover as soon as her first lover has paid a certain amount of the marriage price to her father or brother. Duels will follow sometimes but these are merely an expression of jealousy, rather than a punishment for misbehavior. Sexual intercourse before marriage, or even between lovers who do not contemplate marriage, is not considered wrongful but is called "stealing." "Stealing" is a question of opportunity, and opportunism is one of the principal elements in their moral standard.

The worst feature of the burial tradition is that it will take generations to exterminate this practice, because it has become part and parcel of their natural instincts. I am told that it is much easier to convert the Wakikuyu to religion than to bury their dead, for, although they will discard their code in favor of the European principles, still they will hold on tenaciously to their method of undertaking. Every time a Christian dies there is the same struggle for the last rites of Christianity. In some cases the more advanced Wakikuyu make an exception, especially when the father of three or more sons is concerned, and when the sons have worked in European communities as soldiers or servants. Under such circumstances the boys will take the consequences rather than face the scorn of their employers or companions, who are members of other tribes, and they will bury their father in a decent manner. But even here there must be a purifying ceremony for ten days, during which they must not come in contact with the outer world and banish all effects of the contact with the dead by a long series of cleansings, routine sacrifices, absolutions, and solitary confinement. This burial takes place only where a father has three or more sons who are all circumcised and are in good standing with the community.

I had always been interested in the psychology of dancing. Dancing to me is a language of signs and an expression of sentiments of the emotional side of the man and the woman. It interprets the language of the soul where words would be too familiar and expression too risqué.

I have never danced myself and probably for this reason imagine more psychological value in this particular than there really is, but I see more in the impulsive characteristics of races in a dance than I can notice in their languages or national characteristics; as a matter of fact, I judge their characteristics often from their dances.

I may be wrong and yet I feel that watching a dance is the surest criterion by which to confirm other impressions. It even shows their standard of social intercourse among one race. A visit to seaside and summer resorts will uphold my theory in this matter better than any other argument. The very music tells its tale.

The dance is to a certain extent the moral index of the tribe and this generalization is especially true with the Wakikuyu. Among the Wanyika, it will be remembered the funeral dance is the principal and most solemn ceremony after the death of a member of the tribe and a direct call is made to the young women of the tribe to keep the clan in existence. Among the Wakamba there is the witch dance to invoke death on a troublesome member of the tribe. Among the Wakikuyu the conception of the dance carries more of a spirit of pride for past and present deeds of valor. This idea pervades the whole dance and the whole series of passes and figures in the dance serve as it were to demonstrate what the participants have done or are able to do.

The dance begins with an exhibition by about twenty young warriors, all circumcised, who walk about in a brave manner as though to defy any challenger. They are in full war paint and carry their heads high. At given intervals they stop their march around the field and indulge in a monotonous pass in which they shake their heads up and down carefully tossing their long hair back from the forehead.

They go through this movement defiantly staring straight ahead and ignoring all onlookers; then in a measured step they stalk about apparently unmindful of the audience but aware of their physical attractions which elicit a certain amount of deserved admiration from the women. They wear a sword by their sides to proclaim that at any time they are ready and willing to defend not only the tribe but their lady loves. They have eyes for no one except the maidens who are the chief witnesses of their prowess.

When the crowd is gathered around, other young warriors stand about the circle in a group of their own, each holding his spear manfully, with his sword drawn. When the spectators have warmed up to the occasion each outside group in turn runs about the field circling the main dancing party and making a killing display in front of the girls who applaud them, sometimes merely shouting their admiration, sometimes by running after the single dancers bearing a little twig in their hands. The young warrior, who poses here with drawn sword must have killed a man, a Masai, or a Mukamba with his own weapon before he is allowed to make this exhibition. He brandishes his weapon in the air with pride and glory, and the more the women proclaim his bravery, the wilder become his antics. He looks about for his lady love, hoping to outshine his brothers in her eyes. At present this display is merely a ceremony because the British Government has prohibited the promiscuous killing of enemies. However the tradition lasts and the girls take the will for the deed.

Presently there arrive on the scene other young warriors who proudly carry their shields. They take their turns at a pass which is even wilder than that of their preceding competitors. They form a corner of their own in the field and it is evident that the young women are not cold to them, as the furtive glances at the newcomers soon become less shy. Once the warriors consider the women's attention sufficiently aroused they dart out into the middle of the arena and start a sham fight with their spears and swords, protecting themselves with their gorgeously painted shields. Every muscle is taut and all eyes are on the alert for a parry. They lunge at one another, each trying to drive his spear home. They run around for a favorable opening, harassing their opponents as much as they dare, until they are able to drive them back and out of the field. The girls now have no interest in the dancers,

WAKIKUYU "NGOMA" DANCE
Just completed their costume, Lava stockings the feature.
Their bronze muscular bodies shine in the sun
First pass of the dance.

SOCIAL LIFE IN WAKIKUYU
Group of Wakikuyu debutantes watching the dance
Social scions decked out to catch the ladies' fancy
A covy of Wakikuyu flirts

but follow every movement of the fighters. The conquering hero is applauded and showered with smiles and flattery. His physical charms are discussed by the fair ones who vie with one another to catch a glimpse of the hero.

Then another bid is made by the spearman for further favors from the women and now they begin a free for all fight in which all comers are welcome. They prance around the arena like wild men and in the confusion they frequently come into unexpected contact with one who is not at that moment their immediate opponent and wheeling around they attack the newcomer. Those who are driven out of a certain prearranged line are considered "hors de combat" and must withdraw unless he become embroiled with another warrior who is within the limits. However, there is little doubt as to their skill and courage in the minds of the girls and the other spectators. No wreath or crown is placed upon their brows for their reward is to come later, when the women have had ample opportunity to pass upon all the assorted feats of gallantry exhibited by the warriors and dancers. That part of the "ngoma" does not arrive until the last hour before sundown.

The dance "goes merrily on" while the men who are greased with sheep fat and red lava dust, decorated with a variety of feathers, local animal tails, heads, chains, rings, belts, and adorned with everything except clothes, begin to perspire profusely, and the mixture runs down their backs and chests. But their merriment knows no fatigue nor intermission and their endurance is worthy of admiration. The rays of the afternoon sun beat mercilessly on their oil-drenched skins, which would make any man but a native of this soil collapse. It makes one dizzy to watch the dancers move their owl-like heads backwards and forwards with sudden jerks that would cause concussion of the brain in a white man. But perhaps the native brain requires a thorough shaking up to put it on a level with the human variety.

The most amusing part of their corporeal decorations of war paint probably is their imitation stockings. It is diverting to watch the natives don their pedal finery. They go to a stream or water hole long before the dance begins and, provided with a piece of decayed lava or pumice stone, they apply the wetted material to the calves of their legs and draw all manner of fanciful patterns with their finger nails. There are no traditional designs, and every dancer is his own architect. They look like owls in the green masks which they daub on their faces. The visage, surrounded by a wig of natural hair, arranged in two inch coils of the smallest possible diameter, and smeared in sheep fat and lava dust, with their small beady eyes gleaming out, are a sight for the evil spirits to behold. The stoical look in their eyes gives them the appearance of a host of spirits such as Dante describes in his "Inferno." The "tout ensemble" of this heterogeneous crowd dancing around is a revelation which only beholders of a Kikuyu "ngoma" may enjoy.

The peak of the dance is reached only when the girls join in the chorus. Here is the apotheosis of the "ngoma." The girls have had ample opportunity to choose the winner— "their man," as it were. The warriors by this time have no doubt as to their choice and the maidens also are very definite about their predilections. There is an intermission in which each "beau" edges up to his "belle." The young lady looks radiantly on her "beau," the young warrior returns her glance with interest, and so the cast for the "grand finale" is made up. There is no artificiality in this selection for it is Nature herself who determines the plan for the continuation of the "genus humanum" so far as the Wakikuyu are concerned.

"Choose your partner" is the unspoken command, and the young folks are not slow to obey. When all the dancers and the gladiators and their mates are gathered they form a ring in the center of which the leading beauties are assembled. These lead a song in praise of the warriors and the surrounding chorus join with them to intone the motif of the passes of the dance. The young men and the young women are face to face, the hands of the women being placed lightly on the hips of the men. No suggestive motions are made. They merely dance a slow step, beating time to their own singing, and increasing the time as they proceed. They bring both feet flat on the ground and the great crowd is silent as the earth trembles under their feet. They all throw up their hands and clap them time and time again above their heads. This is a very interesting part of the ceremony, and adds to the color of the dance. The crowd around them look on with a certain jealousy which does not escape the white man who watches the dancers. The emotion is justified because the participants of the "round dance" are picked men and women of their country. The older women are sorry that their time is past (as soon as girls are married they abstain from taking part in the dance). The older men feel the stiffening of their limbs more acutely now than ever. The younger generation of both sexes are eagerly waiting for the time to come in which they shall have their fling.

It is noteworthy also that the men especially show a remarkable physique, lithe and slim, with every muscle alert and mobile. They are steady and sure in their movements, displaying a grace which is not diminished by their savage surroundings. The girls are coy in their demeanor and gentle in their poise; their diffidence in the crowd demonstrates as under no other circumstances the inherent gentility of their character. In a word there is no objectionable feature in any part of the dance, which might be shown in the most puritanical society without giving Mrs. Grundy any excuse to denounce the great Wakikuyu pastime.

While I prefer to watch their tribal traditions and customs I do not overlook the commercial traits of the character and in the case of the Kikuyu this was forced upon me more or less in a dramatic manner. In talking to one of the prominent officials, I found that the

Government objected very strongly to the dances for economical reasons. This same question was later emphasized by an English functionary. Shortly after we had our dance, the "lid" was put on tight.

One character trait which sets the Wakikuyu above the average East African negro is his thrifty, industrial spirit. His energy and willingness to work for a living is so pronounced that "ngomas" must be held on Sundays, for all other days are working days. The Wakikuyu crops are planted and tended with care, and when the harvest comes, the natives make certain that the birds do not harvest the fruits of their labor. They do not entrust the protection of their crops to scarecrows, so they send their boys and girls into the fields from six o'clock to eight in the morning and again from four o'clock to six in the evening. During the period preceding the harvest, you will hear the hills and valleys ring with the sound of the children's voices, screaming and shouting to keep the birds away. The children are equipped with a sling, and when vocal warnings are insufficient, stones and lumps of earth ward off winged intruders.

Coffee growing is the principal industry of the Wakikuyu at the present time, and the

WAKIKUYU CUSTOMS

A living scarecrow in Wakikuyu

Wakikuyu warriors at the dance for admiration of the girls

PROFESSIONS
Wakamba snake charmers training to become medicine men
Wanyika heralds announce the funeral dance

boys and girls participate actively in this occupation. Thousands of Wakikuyu are employed in picking berries during the harvest, and during the growing season they are constantly clearing the ground and weeding. There are some coffee plantations which employ three hundred Wakikuyu all year 'round. The natives shell the beans, dry them and store them—all without the supervision of an overseer. After their day's work, which ends at four in the afternoon, the natives return home to work their own garden patches or banana plantations.

The youngsters tend the flocks of sheep and goats, while the older boys look after the herds of cattle. One rarely sees young warriors unemployed or idling about. Even if the Wakikuyu are somewhat remiss in learning or adopting Christianity, at least they practice the gospel of labor. They are not expert mechanics or artisans, although I have seen infrequent pieces of woodcarving which did them great credit.

It is not likely that they will adopt European methods of work nor do they care much for "modern" methods. They continue to wear their own styles of dress and look down on the young bloods who ape the fashions of the white men. I heard one missionary say that the Wakikuyu would give ninety percent of their possessions if the white men would depart from their country and leave the natives to do things in their own way. And this opinion came from one who is the best loved and most respected white man among them, a man who has been with them for twenty-five years.

The traveler is surprised at the extreme sense of modesty which these people have developed—especially the women. I noted this in connection with their dance, but their modesty is not confined to any special occasion and there seems to be nothing artificial about it. No matter where one happens on the Wakikuyu women, they are always well dressed—or shall I say well covered? Unlike the women of other tribes, the Wakikuyu do not fancy European styles of dress but retain the severe customs of their ancestors. The traditional wardrobe consists of three pieces of skin, one to cover the breasts, one to protect the back—this piece practically encircles the body —and one, a sort of small apron skirt, which begins at the waist. This last skin is never removed, even when the wearer is bathing in the stream. The first two may occasionally be abandoned when the women are working hard and the heat becomes oppressive, but the apron, which is a small triangular bit of goat-skin, is looked upon almost as a fetish, the removal of which would pollute a woman's soul for all time. The large skin—the mantle—is a garment of small skins sewed together. All of the skins are continually soaked in castor oil and lava dust, which not only makes them pliable, but which also serves as a signal that the wearer is approaching, owing to the sound produced by the contact and rubbing of the skins. This system of dress is not altogether agreeable to the nostrils, although it is not quite as offensive in this respect as the costume of the Wakamba women.

The women also wear a great variety of trinkets which serve to adorn their heads, necks, arms and legs. It would be futile to enumerate all of them, if not, indeed, impossible, for one finds new ornaments every day. An almost universal decoration consists of three tiny sticks placed in three holes punctured in the upper part of the ear-shell. A whole collection of earrings, an inch and a half in diameter, made of pink, blue and white beads, hang from an aperture in the lower part of the ear lobe. This aperture is quite large and widely extended. Sometimes a wooden ring is worn in the lobe and the rings suspended from the wood. The hole in the lobe may be from two and a half to three inches in diameter, so that it sometimes serves as a receptacle for a bottle.

Necklaces of beads are another popular decoration. Some of these trinkets contain sixty or seventy strings of beads and they are rather burdensome neckwear for a young girl. Coils of brass, iron, and copper rings about the arms and the calves of the leg are common. Strings of beads make effective head bands, but they are worn only at dances. Wristbands, similarly constructed, are in great demand and some of them are genuinely artistic creations. These seem to be derived from the bands which the natives have seen on European wrist watches. It would be impossible to list all of the gewgaws which the Wakikuyu men and women wear in their ears. Key rings, key handles, army buttons, chains—the catalogue is long. The most peculiar ornament I saw was a broken compass, minus the crystal and the needle, but with the dial intact.

Hairdressing is an art with the Wakikuyu that might be studied profitably by American tonsorial specialists. Girls of marriageable age (13-16) find it essential to shave the head, leaving a central crown of about four inches in diameter dripping with castor oil and lava dust, the hair plaited minutely, like old-fashioned lace curtain fringes, with an enticing circle of oily red drippings about the crown. The eyelashes are clean shaven or extracted— and they are just as particular about this operation as the New York business man is said to be about his morning shave. The warriors and dancers also are finicky about their hairdressing, so that they may cut an imposing figure in the dance. The hair must be just so long and no longer in order to achieve the full effect involved in shaking the mane up and down and back and forward during the dance. The very young and the very old care little about hairdressing. Before and after they are in the dancing group, they do not matter socially.

One of the most surprising discoveries I made was a ceremony of private confession among the Kikuyu pagans, a rite very similar to the Sacrament of Penance in the Catholic Church. Sin, among the Wakikuyu, is believed to be the source of all evil and unless the sin is remitted and forgiven, it is bound to result in death or in some great misfortune. Consequently, when a pagan has committed a sin, he goes to the medicine man and confesses his misdeed to that grandee, who is thought to be able to appease the spirit of vengeance. Sin is not necessarily a transgression of the moral code of the decalogue, but a violation of any traditional virtue or custom of the tribe. Sins against the law of nature are regarded with particular horror while moral transgressions which are "natural" are likely to be condoned. Therefore, it is with confessions of sins against nature that the native will seek the ear of the medicine man. There are unpardonable sins; incest and bestiality. So great is this conviction that not long ago a girl who was sinned against by her father, who was drunk at the time, committed suicide by drowning in the Chaina River. Although the poor girl was not consciously or even morally guilty of the crime, she was so ashamed and so fearful of the consequences of the act that she ended her life to propitiate the spirit of decency. Sins of bestiality are partly propitiated by killing the animal which was responsible for the violation of nature's law.

Transgressions of tribal *"mores"* may be adjusted by the confessional. The breach may be altogether harmless morally and yet it may offend the spirit which guards the purity of the tribe. For instance, there is turpitude in-

AFRICAN TYPES

Wakamba coiffure of the masculine genius
Masai type of warrior
Boy with elongated head. Skull is shaped in youth

PROPITIATORY SACRIFICE OF THE WAKIKUYUS
A white kid is sacrificed as peace offering in a feud
Friends of the assaulted party helping him eat the find

volved when the wind blows away the thatch of a roof at night or when the wind whisks off a man's clothing, leaving him nude. A hyena entering the village courtyard or a jackal barking in the public square are forms of sin. Such events although void of human guilt, must be atoned for by the victim, who goes to the medicine man, confesses his violation of tribal integrity and is absolved after paying his sacrifice of a goat to the medicine man.

Sometimes, when a personal sin is concerned, the penitent may be so diffident about his revelation that he cannot overcome his confusion and the medicine man will hand him a stick, bidding him confess to the piece of wood. The man steps aside, whispers his story to the stick, turns the stick over to the medicine man, who casts away the wood, saying, "There go your sins." A goat is presented to the wizard —and all is well.

There are happenings which are not in themselves sinful but which are considered evil auguries and these, too, are confessed. As an example, a man may be on his way to another village and encounter a snake on the road. Immediately he turns back; for he looks on the incident as an expression of the unwillingness of the spirit to permit him to proceed, and if he is especially worried he may go to the medicine man and the spell is banished by the sacrifice of a goat. When a woman throws a lump of earth at her husband, the act is taken to mean that she despises him and he asks for a divorce. Her exhibition of contempt is considered an omen of the displeasure of the spirits and the man may go to the medicine man to have the curse removed. Whether he confesses or not, the divorce invariably is granted.

The confession is known as "taika" which means to "vomit" or "cause vomiting." The doctrine is a logical corollary of the philosophy which sways the Wakikuyu. The contagion of the evil effect of sin is entirely personal or confined to the family of the transgressor. There is no fear that outsiders may be infected, but the contagion may strike any one who is connected with the original offender. Forgiveness for touching a corpse may be obtained by confession if the deed was done accidentally.

There is a system of confession which is practiced when a person is in danger of death. The sick man calls the medicine man to his side and has the medicine skin placed on the ground. The wizard enters solemnly, with measured step. He slowly deposits gourds filled with magic powders and grains on the skin. He then passes his hand or a Kongoni horn (the Kongoni or Hartebeest is supposed to impart especial reviving influences, being the symbol of powerful vitality) over the patient's face and neck. This is done to determine whether or not there is enough vitality left in the patient to hold out hopes of recovery. Now he mixes certain powders and gives them to the sick man to swallow. All of these treatments have their symbolical and even pathological meaning. He watches the effect of the medicine—and looks wise. Presently he takes four twigs with leaves on them and places two of them under the patient's arms. He passes the remaining two through the aperture in the patient's ear lobes and then throws the sticks behind his back. The sticks under the arms meeting at his back shows there is still sufficient strength left in the heart. The sticks passed through the earlobes, if they meet at the base of the cranium, demonstrate that there is still a certain powerful action left in the nervous center. This ritual also expels the evil spirit from the patient's soul.

With the departure of the evil spirit, the effects of the spirit's tenancy are treated. The sick man is compelled to take a mouthful of the desiccated contents of a goat's stomach, which he spits out. This measure also has a diagnostic effect for if the stomach can retain this mess it shows that his digestive organism is still in good condition, as indeed it must be. We must recall that "taika" is vomiting. The patient is now considered pure, and ready to have his fate pronounced over him. The augury is read by the medicine man from two groups of pebbles, beans and buttons, which he shakes out of a small gourd and deposits on the cow skin. He counts the two groups and if the nearer group is the greater, it means that there is no hope for the sufferer. Hereupon, the unfortunate's friends take him to a cleared space in the brush, where he is laid down gently to await death. The same friends gather a few branches and leaves and construct a shade over him, leaving the front open so that the hyenas will easily find the remains. A little fire is built to provide the poor man with the last comforts and to protect him against the cold night air, and he is left to drag out his last hours of misery as best he may. If the waiting is prolonged, his friends and relations may occasionally visit him and offer delicacies, but usually the mental depression following the pronouncement of doom, causes him to turn over and die without

A WAKIKUYU ENGAGEMENT

This native told Dr. Vanden Bergh that he had just become engaged to the finest little girl in the world. His spear is sheathed
with a plume to show that his intentions are peaceful. The girl
by carrying his spear accepts his proposal.

CARRYING THE COFFEE CROP TO MARKET

a struggle. Many cases of autothanatos have thus been known to occur.

Contrary to all traditions of other tribes and countries, marriage seems to be an event of sorrow rather than an occasion for joy in Kikuyu. I have noted previously that when a Kikuyu maiden is in love with a man she changes her attitude towards him as soon as he has proposed marriage and has paid part of the marriage price. She then looks upon him as her lord and master and takes another lover. This paradox becomes even more startling after the nuptials have been completed.

Of course there is a mutual understanding between the bride and the bridegroom before the great event "which holds the world enthralled" is consummated. That very understanding has prompted the future husband to visit the maiden's father or older brother, bringing a few gourds of beer, and under the influence of a friendly drink, to discuss matters and to come to an agreement as to the price of the woman in the case. Forty to sixty goats are the usual price of the young man's "passion divine." He loses no time in paying down the first installment of ten goats, and the non-return of these is a sign that the only-girl-in-the-world has accepted him officially and that the wedding may take place as soon as he has paid off the rest of the dowry. Six or eight months pass before he has paid in full, and then he awaits his opportunity to carry off his bride by main strength.

To capture the bride he sends three of his friends to waylay the girl at a certain prearranged spot which she is known to frequent— usually near the village or at the well. When the coast seems clear, the young men seize her and she raises the conventional "hue and cry." She resists and struggles in the most approved maidenly manner, but her efforts are, of course, fruitless. No one comes to her rescue, and presently she is borne away to the groom, who awaits her in high glee. He carries her off to his mother's hut, while she fights back and weeps continually. After she has been placed in the hut, she weeps for eight days more, while her husband remains away. Actual tears are shed, and old timers in this country maintain that the thought of being made a slave prompts this lachrymal outburst, but I fancy that the tears are caused by no very serious emotion. Be that as it may, after a week of frenzied crying, the girl returns home to her mother. She seems a humiliated soul, groaning and walking with weary steps. She remains with her mother for part of the day, and then her husband calls for her. The girl has the option of asking her father to return the goats and the other items of the dowry, in which case no marriage is established.

For ten days the husband has lived apart from her, but when she returns with her master to his mother's hut, there is no further excuse for delay in the consummation of the marriage. That night they become man and wife in fact, and she may no longer run away from her husband unless divorce has set her free. The bride's girl friends come and make a great display of sorrow on losing their playmate. They stay for three days, during which period they weep endlessly. When they are gone, the young couple start life in earnest and the husband sets about the business of building his own hut and establishing his own family.

After marriage the woman no longer is entitled to attend dances or other festivities, but must work to enrich her husband and look after his interests. For her marriage has been a real burial of all her privileges and of her freedom of action. Perhaps, she has had reason to weep at the thought of ending her girlhood. And yet—to remain a spinster at eighteen is considered a disgrace among the

Wakikuyu and women who are unmarried at that age are put in the same category with the defiled and the uncircumcised.

The rest of the Wakikuyu customs are similar to those of the Wakamba and other native tribes, except in a few details. The native villages resemble those of the Wakamba, and there are as many huts as there are wives in the chief's harem. Each wife keeps her own children with her and tends them. There are granary huts for each wife and the chief has a storehouse of his own. There is a little "boma" for the cattle, the sheep and the goats. Each head of a family starts his own village and when the young men marry they start their own establishments. Although the huts are small, there are partitions for the girls and boys, with a private apartment for the mother and father. The grown-up boys sleep wherever they may find a resting place, although sometimes there is a spare hut known as a "house for boys," which also accommodates over-night visitors. When a close friend calls on the chief, the latter will assign him to a certain hut and this hospitality entails the use of the wife whose hut has been placed at the visitor's disposal. She virtually becomes the

EXTREMES OF AGE

Aged Wakikuyu woman. Wanyika girls at the wash tubs

A PEACEFUL VILLAGE IN WAKIKUYU

friend's temporary wife. If a child should be born to the wife and friend, it is considered the property of the chief.

The Wakikuyu have two religions—private and public. The private worship is dedicated to the ancestral spirits of members of the tribe and takes place in their own villages and huts. For public ceremonies, such as sacrifices to obtain rain, the villagers from miles around gather about a sacred tree or grove of trees, which is their temple. The sacred tree is the Mogumo and it is regarded as so sacred by the natives, that any irreverence visited upon it by outsiders is resented by the whole tribe. We discovered this fact when we asked some of the natives to hold a sacrificial ceremony under one of the trees for our benefit. We volunteered to supply the goat for the sacrifice, but they were indignant at our proposition.

"How would you white men like to have us come to your Church," the elder demanded, "and ask you to perform your services to satisfy our curiosity?"

The argument was conclusive, and we had to be content with a still picture of the sacred tree.

The Mogumo is an integral part of their

philosophy of sin and traditional command-
ments. No man dare offend it at the peril of
his life because the transgression will be punished even if the offense remains unknown.
The spirit of the tree is as omnipotent and
omniscient to the natives as that of Zeus was to
the ancient Greeks.

Circumcision is prevalent with the Wakikuyu, as it is with most of the African tribes.
The uncircumcised are as pariahs, and no girl
would think of marrying an uncircumcised
young man, or vice versa. This ceremony
admits the boy to the rank of warrior and the
girl to the marriageable state. The rite in the
Kikuyu country carries with it obligations of
taboo, and when a young man considers the
taboo of the Kikuyu rite an imposition which
he does not care to obey, or when there are too
many species of viands of which he may not
partake, he asks leave to be circumcised according to the Masai custom. The medicine man
converts him to that order, and no distinction
is made in admitting him to all the privileges
of the Kikuyu tribe. The circumcision of
boys is not entirely completed, only three-
fourths of the foreskin being removed. Formerly, warriors would not be considered full-

grown men, even after circumcision, unless they had killed a member of a hostile tribe. The ceremony used to be followed by head hunting expeditions consisting of ten or more braves, but the criminal code imposed by the British Government has ended this practice.

THE MASAI

IT is remarkable how nature itself directs the separation of races and tribes and prescribes their boundaries through tribal instincts and desires, giving each what they ask for as suiting their inclinations best. It is an open question whether frontiers are made by geographic limitations as much as by ethnical considerations or rather the racial cravings and requirements. Or whether the surroundings and environment of the races once placed have decided their cultural tastes and shaped their tribal wants in the selection of primordial modes of living. Why are pastoral tribes and why their agricultural counterparts? Did the tribes select their territories or did territories determine their needs and tastes? One may argue either way or other and support his conclusions with equally strong arguments pro and con. The question would merely lead to a "circulus vitiosus." It is the old problematical "was the egg or the hen first" enigma.

That question intruded itself on my mind more than any other on passing the boundary line between the Kikuyu and the Masai. There was only a distance of a hundred odd miles between the two centers which I had picked out for a study of the two tribes. From Mangu we returned south to the city of Nairobi where, crossing the Uganda Railroad, we moved another sixty miles due south to the best Masai settlement which offered. Leaving Nairobi there was only a thin narrow slip of fertile soil to pass before we crossed into an ideal pasture land. The dividing line between red lava deposit of the North and the gray and black loam undulations of the South was so marked that it left an indelible impression on my memory which comes to the foreground whenever I think of the two races. The foothills leading to the heights of Mount Kenia became smaller until they almost settled into the corrugations of the vast grazing lands of the Masai.

Is the local aspect of the bleak prairie responsible for the almost sour and certainly bloodthirsty nature of the Masai as contrasted against the gentle nature of the green garden fed indigène of the always higher climbing Kikuyus? Or is it the dietary effect of the

staples of the territories? Traditional enemies
of ages they live without ever a thought of
settling in the domains invaded and conquered
in the many raids they mutually made on each
other. Now then, is it the innate instinct of
race, or the effect of territorial propensities in
the form of nourishment which forms so different a human being at so short a distance?
And above all why should the Masai disdain
vegetables and mealies and live on meat, blood
and milk exclusively whilst their neighbors, the
"Kyuks," crave for both? I leave the solution to the Ethnologist and the Dietitian to
settle, for I confess the problem passes beyond
my ken.

It is sufficient to say here that the economic
expert looking at the country from a merely
commercial standpoint hastened a branch line
into the coffee producing country to the north
and did not even cut a decent wagon road into
the south without speculating as to the why
and wherefor. And to tell the truth I made
our stay in the Masai country as short as I con-
veniently could and hurried our operations
with the utmost speed in order to get away
from so inhospitable a country where one
could not even get a drink of water without
swallowing germs so self-asserting that they

made themselves almost felt crawling on the
palate and where only living creatures of the
coarsest kind seemed to have survived. To
grapple with that element and thrive seems
impossible and that probably explains the
vanishing condition of the Masai since when
man is pitched against the coarsest of beasts
the outcome is no longer a question of surmise.

So at last the time had come to visit the
"Masai." The redoubtable fame of the Masai
was almost as well established among the white
men in British East Africa and Uganda as
that of the Mohicans of our Red Indians, and
in mentioning this comparison I might add
that it will not be long before some historian
will write a book on the "Last of the Masai."
I was not prepared for the disappointment I
had in store for me from the beginning. The
Masai had given the Government so much
trouble that they had been driven back to a
reservation into which no white man was
allowed to go without a permit. This regulation was strictly adhered to by Mr. Ainsworth,
the Natives Commissioner of Nairobi. The
fact that my contemplated lion hunt with
spears by the Masai had been adversely criticized by the local journal of Nairobi did not
make my efforts to pass the border line easier.

However, the American Consul, Mr. Eells, sponsored me and that gave my expedition an entrée.

I shall not soon forget that trip. I was told that the journey could be made by automobile and consequently I had chartered a car for ourselves and a couple of mule wagons for the saffari.

The road was very good for about twenty-five miles. I had been given a very vague idea of the distance and the road but the farther we proceeded the more complicated reports became. Finally arriving at Ngong, the Government Station, I was told that the nearest settlement was at least thirty miles away. The Masai shift their locations so frequently that no one seemed to know where to look for them, consequently our directions were very vague.

Striking out from the road to the south we drove our car into the open veld and soon got entangled in all sorts of obstacles, dry creek beds covered with big bowlders and rock croppings on the plains. An amusing sight were the herds of Grants, Kongoni and Thompsons, varieties of buck which stood at attention ears up and eyes directed our way. Then the leader would turn away and lead his flock into safer regions, himself falling back to act as rear-guard protector. The Kongoni were the last and hardest to move, protesting, as it were, to have their peaceful possession invaded.

We got stuck in one of the creek beds about fifty-five miles out of Nairobi and my Masai guide whom I had taken out of Ngong assured me that we were near Anguruya's kraal. I marched ahead following my guide and at last after a march over undulating ground I saw across the next creek a circle of low dime-loaf-shaped huts surrounded by a thorn hedge— but not a soul in sight. I ranged my powerful glasses on the village but not a figure could I see nor any signs of cattle by which the Masai villages are always known. "Not a living soul there," said I to my guide.

"Kulala" (sleep) answered he in broken Kiswahili at the same time urging me on.

While I could not distinguish a sign of life our movements evidently had been noticed because coming down the slope I soon detected three or four tall figures armed with spears shining in the sun, coming our way. I knew then that my quest had not been in vain.

The tall spearmen came to a standstill in front of us. The leader accosted my guide, ignoring me. An exchange of greetings ensued carried on by the villagers whose answering monosyllables of "Ah ah," "eh eh," "oh oh," in monotonous succession fascinated me until at the end of my guide's harangue the chief (Anguruya himself) came up to me, spat on his hand and held it out to me. He led us into the village, the two warriors falling in line behind me.

Having learned more of our intentions on the way to the village, he conducted me into the kraal and with a sweep of his long arm and long nailed fingers he bade me welcome with "the village is yours."

Presently he dived into two or three of the cow-manure plastered huts, and introduced me to his four wives whom he had brought out. "They are yours," he said, "and you may pick out whatever hut you please or these," pointing to the women, "will build your own hut (meaning my tent), if you prefer."

I thanked him for the kind offer but told him that I would not trespass on his liberal and welcoming offer.

The women looked at me and took one of my white hands admiring its color and another took off my hat and pointed to my glossy smooth hair, exposing my dome to the dangerous rays of the sun. I smiled, putting back

MASAI VILLAGE LIFE

Village of the plains. Huts are plastered with cowmanure

Thornbush gate is opened in the morning to let out cattle

Masai women in "dolce far mente"

A MASAI HERDER IN FAVORITE REST POSE

my hat, and made a sign of thirst giving utterance to the word "madzi." They giggled and looked askance at my guide and presently one of the ladies dived into a hut and brought out a gourd of grayish looking, evil smelling fluid. Thirsty as I was I put the gourd to my lips taking care to let the water drop out on the ground. While I did not let a drop of it pass my lips my nostrils got the full benefit of the stench.

Presently my companions came in and I introduced them to the chief and his court. The "freedom of the city" was conferred upon them in the same gentle and liberal fashion and presently we settled down.

To describe the Masai one must look at them from an altogether different standpoint than that from which we have thus far considered the other races. They are a purely pastoral and Hamitic tribe, speaking a Nilotic language, wherein they differ in all essentials from the Wakamba, Wanyika and Wakikuyu. A pastoral tribe is naturally void of all central settlement and home comforts for the reason that it is always traveling and leads a nomadic life. The Masai are as might be and has been said, on a continuous "saffari." True, there is a certain proportion of the elders who stay at home and have villages, but even these travel from place to place and frequently it occurs that they establish themselves in three or four different villages in one year. This happens particularly when there is a cattle disease which they try to escape by moving about, avoiding the grasses which have been saturated with the germs of the dying cattle. Sometimes they overcome a disease in this manner.

It will be seen, then, that there is a valid reason why the Masai are a tribe about which little can be said with regard to their domestic habits—for they are not a domestic people. They have no pottery, no basketry, no blacksmiths, no grain fields or any sort of agriculture nor any other kind of industry for the reason that whatever they need they buy. Being a Spartanlike stoical race they have reduced their needs to the most rudimentary requirements of nature disdaining all artificial supplements to living comfort. They are rich in cattle, some of which they acquire in raids, and, with their war-like dispositions, they are the most dreaded tribe in East Africa.

All they look for when they do settle down is water and plenty of range with the best kind of grass for their cattle. Their villages, when they build them, are of the crudest kind and planned more for the convenience and safe protection of their cattle than for themselves. They set up a number of huts in a circular form with a hedge of rough thorn brush surrounding the circle, high and thick enough to prevent the wild animals from clearing the fence. There are certain open spaces left in the hedge so that the cattle can come in and go out in the mornings and evenings. These openings in the thorn walls are closed every night when the cattle have come home and they are reopened in the morning. There is a peculiar superstition connected with this opening and closing. No one is permitted to open or shut them out of time for fear that the spirits of the tribal forefathers will be offended at being shut out. We wished to take a picture of the operation in daylight, but this was the only thing which the chief, Anguruya, had to refuse us and his apologies were profuse, but we respected the idea and took the picture in the early morning when the doors were officially opened.

The interior of the village is laid out entirely with a view to accommodate the cattle. There is an inner circle surrounded by a similar hedge of thornbrush with gates which also are closed at night and opened in the morning.

This enclosure is put up so that the cattle may be herded together. The circle is proportioned according to the number of cattle it is intended to shelter, and it is left open overhead without any covering whatsoever. The accumulation of cow manure is enormous for the space is never cleaned or cleared. Of course the Masai have a great many usages for this commodity for they all but eat it. They use it as medicine, as fuel, as plaster for their huts, and even for chairs. Not seldom does one find that the center of the cattle enclosure is higher than the top of the hedge surrounding it, and sometimes there is an elevation of two feet of ground on the inside of the hedge projecting above the outside level.

The construction material of the whole village consists of twigs and branches of trees of the thinnest kind, owing to the fact that the Masai always live in parts of the country where there is scarcely any forest or wooded area. They seek the pori country because there the best grass usually is found. For miles and miles around there is not one tree which gives shade enough to relieve the midday heat, except around the edges of riverbeds and creeks. Consequently, the Masai use light twigs for the frames of their houses. The rest of the building material is plentiful because it is cow-dung. And to be truthful, it is the best plaster to be found because it is pliable and goes through the cracks of the frame easily and it goes there to stay. They use tons and tons of it. It is antiseptic, killing germs which otherwise would be plentiful in a village where the natives are so unsanitary and unclean. The odor which would be repugnant to white men is perfume to the Masai. When thoroughly dried it is waterproof, for they do not allow the cracks and splits to widen before filling up the gaps. The outer finish is smooth and even, and a thick application covers the whole building so that in case of rain the water easily runs down.

The interior of the hut is as crude as the outside. The entrance—for one may not call it a door—is about four feet high, so that one must stoop to enter. It is so narrow that one must slide in sideways rather than stoop forward. There is an inside wall, very thin but effective, which separates the home of the young calves from that of the human inhabitants. On the near and far sides of the huts there are two alcoves or built-in bedsteads and maybe a third built up against the front wall if it is desired, to curtail the accommodations of the calves. The space left between these bedsteads holds the fireplace in the center, with squatting room for the members of the family. There are four tiny posts in the center of the hut which may be utilized as chairbacks. There is always a fire smoldering in the grate, or rather, between the three stones which take the place of a grate. The beds remind one of the couches of the early Visigoths and Franks because they are composed of a number of skins and cowhides piled on top of one another. These skins are cured but not tanned so that I cannot vouch for their being a soft couch. The only utensils or substitutes for crockery are long oval gourds used for water and milk. They have no cooking pots of any description because they don't cook mealies or other vegetables. They live entirely on meat and milk. It is said that some of the Masai eat mealies clandestinely only, and that must be so, because I could find no traces of any in the villages which I visited, although I made it a point to look for these elusive articles. For spitirons on which to turn their meat, they use the ever handy twig or perhaps a discarded lower point of a spear; from all of which it will be seen that the Masai live a most primitive life and have very few wants.

Yet they were a hardy race before the entrance of the white man. I use the word "were" advisedly, because since they were forbidden to raid and wage war with their neighbors they have become more indolent and have acquired habits of overindulging in sexual excesses which threaten to destroy the race. The rate of childbirth among them is alarming and it is said by some authorities that there are no more than 20,000 Masai left in the country. This statement was partly borne out by the fact that there were very few children in the villages which we visited. What effect insufficient housing has to do with this condition is a study well worth entering into, because when one considers that their huts are only 14 feet long, 7 feet deep and 6 feet high and a great part of these is occupied by the calves, and that furthermore there is absolutely no light or fresh air to be found in this space, it would seem to argue that there is little chance for the embryo of the human species to develop.

Such mothers as one does find in these villages are extremely proud of their offspring and treat them with the utmost care. I was asked by some of these tender mothers to give them medicines for their children and saw on different occasions where they fed them on butter after weaning. That the youngsters did not like the diet was evident because their mothers would close their tiny nostrils with a lump of butter and force the food down their mouths in large quantities, at which the little beggars balked with arms and legs beating in the air.

The women are a lazy collection, indolent and lackadaisical to a degree. They have nothing to do except build the huts when they change location and to fetch water from the waterholes once or twice a day. The men themselves cook their own meat, roasting and turning it on the fire as they eat. There is no agriculture to keep them busy like the Waki-kuyu and other tribes. They drag their feet along the ground as they walk. This slouch-iness, however, must be explained by the heavy coils of brass and steel wire which they wind about their nether limbs. The coils are flush with the knee and the ankle, and are made of heavy steel wire and polished so that they shine in the sun and dazzle the eye. They cannot weigh an ounce under twelve or thirteen pounds and are absolutely immovable. They are flattened out at the bottom and run a little wider at the knee so as to give that joint a little play. The effect on their feet is dis-

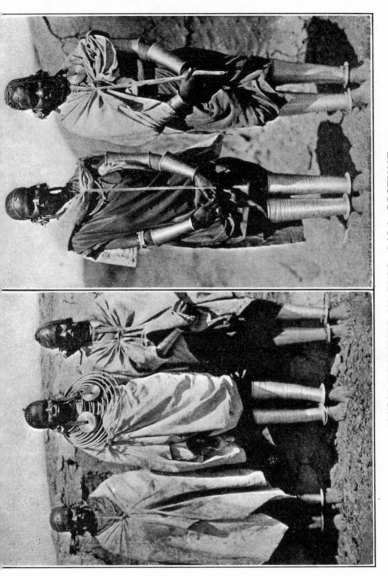

MASAI BEAUTIES IN FULL GALA COSTUME

Steel wire leglets and arm corts weighing from twelve to twenty pounds

JUST WIVES

Masai queens at the investiture of the Chief.
This Mumyika owner of a small harem of four is particular about
his manioc root

astrous in so far that the foot is callous and the skin on the upper part almost as hard as the sole of the feet. They try to protect the upper part of their feet to a certain extent by inserting a rag between the foot and the wire but owing to the heavy weight of these ornaments the soft skin becomes hard nevertheless. They have the same kind of ornamentation for the upper and lower limbs of the arms, although these coils are of a lighter material. The steel wire of which this armlet is made weighs between eight and nine pounds and makes the movements of their arms extremely awkward. The signs of callous can be seen better here than on the feet because there is no protection whatsoever on the wrist and at the upper part of the elbow joint.

Most women sport the coils on the upper and lower right arm and on the lower left arm but in all cases they cover the arm from the elbow down to the wrist. The poor women lag terribly under the heavy weight of these ornaments but they would no more take them off than our ladies would move in society without their trinkets. To make matters worse, they cannot take them off even for a rest or a change occasionally, or when they are sick, but they must carry this dead weight with them from the moment it is put on until the wearer becomes so aged that she can no longer drag the weight.

There is also the necklace of the same size of wire as the leglet. This ornament is twisted in three or four stiff coils about the neck and from the fifth round it widens out until the last coils surround the shoulders. This thing bobs up and down as they walk and when they stoop the spiral comes down over their head surrounding them with as splendid a steel armor as ever the old Frankish warriors wore in battle. This spiral looks very much like a clockspring of enormous size. To complete their ornamentation they have two flat coils of brass, suspended by a strip of rawhide, hanging from the lobes of their ears. These coils hang down on the slope of the neck towards the breasts and sometimes they come down as far as the breasts. Besides these there are a number of other necklaces of beads, turquoise chains and the like. A favorite decoration, for instance, is a rope of small copper chains which they hang in their ears and wind around over their heads. These I have only seen on the favorite wives of the chiefs and they lend the wives the appearance of Egyptian goddesses.

The women's wearing apparel is very much like that of the Wakikuyu—skins which are extremely well tanned and very soft, which softness is increased by the great amount of grease in which they are soaked. The women here, as among the Wakikuyu, are circumcised and wear the little apron of circumcision. They usually wear a piece of Americani or calico for loin cloth and sometimes a mantle of the same material.

The men wear only the short Roman cloak of calico or sometimes of skin, and do not exhibit the slightest modesty about their persons. They wear no ornaments around the arms or legs except a small strip of skin in case they have entered into some agreement with another warrior. They are fond of a string or bracelet of elephant hair or of the tail whiskers of a giraffe with an amulet attached. The reason for their disregard of ornaments is probably to be found in the fact that they cannot be too light on a hunt or in battle where they need all their strength and agility without being weighed down by useless impediments.

One cannot say enough about the great courage of the Masai warriors—which virtue is the only one they claim or care about. To be dubbed a coward among the Masai warriors is sufficient reason to commit suicide or to kill the man who uttered the taunt. Their training is wonderful, and as battle and the chase are their only occupations, they are naturally always in good trim.

The Masai may be said to have a standing army of great military strength and it is amazingly well organized. It is this army which has held the other and surrounding tribes in such great awe of the Masai. The Masai raided and waged war from the coast to the Victoria Lake and their fame as warriors was so far spread that from Mount Kenia to the Kilimanjaro the tribes were in fear and trembling when the news was spread that the Masai were on the warpath in the neighborhood.

The main saffari highways were time and time again threatened by their rebellious outbreaks so that our saffari in 1896, for instance, had to take the German route because the Masai were out for trouble. On such occasions the government closed the main arteries of traffic because they could not undertake the responsibility for attacks from this dreaded tribe. In due course of time the government won out over them but not without many a skirmish and occasional losses.

Owing to the suppression of their raiding proclivities and the gradual closing in of the tribe in certain boundaries of the reservation, the military organization of the Masai has more or less fallen into abeyance so far as martial enterprises are concerned but it is still maintained for hunting and for the continuance of their traditional existence as a warlike tribe.

Their military organization was for all practical purposes a wonderful institution. There were three sections which composed their standing army. The three sections included so many classes or years of circumcision. From this it may be imagined that circumcision and military service were closely interwoven in their effects and causes. Circumcision meant official conscription of the members of the circumcised class. These classes were organized all over the tribe about every four years and became known as the Eletets ages or Pororrs of such and such a name; for instance—Il Kidmei, camp or sirit formations. These camps and sirit formations were apportioned according to geographical location, and they naturally were formed of the different clans or gilata.

The ceremony of the circumcision is known
as the E-unoto ceremony which is called by the
chief medicine man after due consultation of
the spirits and after formal auguries have been
taken. Leaders or Aigwenani are appointed
by the chief medicine man. The appointee is
not notified before the ceremony for fear that
he might do something to disqualify himself.
He in turn appoints two Sirits or Lieutenants
who command their own battalions made up
of the different clans of his geographical location. It often happens that these sirits are
at odds owing to their clan traditions of prowess. This forms the chief source of grief for
the Aigwenani who must use all the diplomacy
at his command to prevent serious misunder-
standings.

If a warrior at the ceremony of his circumcision blinks an eye or shows any sign of pain
he is disqualified and looked upon as a coward
by his comrades and marked for life to such
an extent that he is unable to find a spouse even
after he has killed his man or his lion. Courage is the capital virtue of the Masai; he who
lacks this virtue or flinches at a danger is forever outlawed. After circumcision they always go in pairs and if one runs away from

danger he is reported to the Aigwenani or the
Sirit of his command. Thus, not only the
"esprit de corps" but the morale is kept up to
the highest standard.

Each warrior's shield proclaims to which
sirit and year of circumcision he belongs and
this indicates also his clan and the geographical
section from which he comes.   When the ceremony of the circumcision is over, the day for
the solemn handing over of the country to the
guardianship of the newly made warriors has
arrived.   The principal medicine man, seated
on a chair enthroned on a pile of cowslips, receives them and shakes hands with each warrior as they pass him in review.   On such occasions the married warriors may not leave
their huts while the older and outgoing class is
clothed with old men's garments and stands up
while the younger sit down.   At this time the
chief medicine man addresses the new warriors
and warns them that the safety of their tribe
and country is now in their hands, and that
they must guard it at the cost of their blood
and lives even as their fathers have kept the
country intact and made it possible for them to
become the proud guardians of an unbeaten
and independent race.   After this, each goes

to his own home and gathers his belongings wherewith he departs for the kraal to which his sirit has been assigned.

The older men and outgoing warriors leave the warrior kraal and take up their abode in the kraals of the chief and elders to get married and raise a family. The younger warriors move from place to place as the location of their cattle herds changes. They go out raiding and looking for opportunities to enrich the tribe with new cattle and booty. They concentrate where there is most danger from the wild animals which follow their herds and woe to the man who loses a large number of cattle without giving a good account of himself or warning the warriors of the danger confronting their cattle. Since the government has stopped all raiding, the attention of the Masai is more and more concentrated on the well being of their cattle.

The younger Masai warriors, who live apart from their older clansmen, have corresponding classes of girls, who are of the same circumcision ages, and with whom they live in absolute free love—without being reproved for it. Yet there is a certain sense of honor among them which seems to consider as a virtue abstinence from this promiscuous life. This infor-

mation I had from the chief Anguruya, who
while we were watching the young bucks dance,
told me that every man who went up to the
girls, for whose special benefit this war dance
was given, made it known to these girls that
he was virginal and as yet had not touched a
woman by turning his head over the girl's face
and touching her with his long greasy braids.
It was remarkable how many of the young
men made this a point. That they must be
perfectly truthful about it would be concluded
from the very fact that their fellow warriors
who live in the same kraal with them are called
upon by traditional custom to deny the implied
fact of another's virginity by a statement to
that effect should one of them dare to profess
this virtue without having the right to do so.

There are a number of minor ceremonies
which are performed at different occasions to
celebrate certain events in the lives of the circumcision classes. For instance, there is a feast
when the young warriors, after sufficient time
has been given them to grow their hair into the
warrior's pigtails, depart for their respective
kraals. The outgoing warriors then appear
before their chief with the younger men and
their leader is spat upon by the chief as a blessing. The younger men challenge the older

ones and meet one another in battle until the
older men finally yield to the younger as their
masters at arms. Again, when they used to
go to war, the older men would spill milk and
honey on the ground in token that they would
be victòrious and the women would sprinkle
them with milk from a milk gourd. When the
warriors went to battle and arrived at the place
of combat each fighter planted his spear in the
ground, challenging the enemy, saying that he,
the son of so and so, would not retire but would
die or conquer on that spot. If the enemy
fled, they killed as many as possible. If the
men lingered on the raid, the women, holding
small gourds covered with grass, waited and
prayed for their safe return. The women also
used to keep fresh milk in the gourds for the
refreshment of the warriors when they returned.

When they visit the villages of the elders or
are summoned for a lion hunt in the neighborhood of the elders' village they walk up slowly
and solemnly toward the gate. If the children
know of their coming they go out to meet them
and the warriors lay their hands on the little
heads in solemn silence. They march up to
the gate in a measured step, sober minded and
calm. At the gate of the village the chief re-

ceives them, shaking their hands as the men pass in single file. They then turn toward the huts of the princesses or chief's wives and at a respectful distance await the pleasure of the ladies. They stand at attention with their spears in their hands and their shields resting on the ground. When the ladies finally arrive, the warriors pass from the left to the right shaking hands with them and bidding them welcome. At the end of the salutation the warriors go to the huts of the ladies they know best and plant their spears at the entrance as a token that they are there, without wishing to hide either their identity or the fact of their presence.

They do not eat in these huts nor do they eat at any time with the women, but they seek a spot outside the village near the waterhole or well where they build their fire and grill their own meat. The warriors do not drink anything stronger than milk or water for "fire water" injures their fighting ability. Neither men nor women smoke but they use snuff in great quantities. In the villages of the elders, liquor brewed of sugar cane is very welcome, but it must be smuggled in and used clandestinely as the open use of it is looked upon with great displeasure by the chief who, however, may indulge in it to his heart's content also clandestinely.

For the rest, the Masai have very few habits and customs which are of any importance. Their circumcision is a preparation for the young men to become warriors and they are taught how to shoot birds with their arrows and learn how to throw a bullock, etc. The circumcision itself is accompanied, as in other tribes, with senseless ceremonies. The naming of a child and the funeral ceremonies are also with slight variations similar to those of other tribes and therefore it matters little whether we go farther into these details.

But I part with the Masai with the greatest of regret. It is not only a pity but a shame that so fine a race as the Masai should be doomed to extinction. They are now not only a decadent race but they are on the verge of absolute dissolution as a tribe and as a people. For this there are a number of causes each of which could be avoided with a little organized care. I shall quote three reasons why the Masai are on the decline. The first, no doubt, is the fact that they only marry after the warriors have left the ranks and are settled as old men in the kraals of the elders. The second is that free love amongst the Morans and the

younger generation of women leads to the in-
capacitating of the girls for motherhood. The
third is that there is a steady increase of the
dreaded disease of syphilis among them, owing
to their habits of indolence which were brought
on by the prohibition of raiding and warfare.

It is pitiful to see how few children there are
in the various kraals or villages. The village
in which we stayed for a week was composed
of about thirty huts, each hut representing a
woman of mature age and a wife of a Masai
elder. Of the thirty wives there were only
three who had children under the age of nine.
The chief himself had two children by the four
wives who were living in that particular village. The other twenty wives who were living
elsewhere but always under his control and
consequently unable to have children by other
men, may have been barren or not, but they
could no longer be counted on as producers of
the human race. Furthermore, there were
only five other men in the whole village, among
whom the other women were distributed.
Some of these men were too old to reproduce
and some of the women were also past production.

The younger men and warriors who
visited the village during the lion hunt made

their abode in the huts of the chief's wives and other women's huts which were assigned to them. These warriors enjoy the use of the women whose hut they occupy for the time being, but the children which might be born of such cohabitation never see the light of day out of respect for the elders and the husbands of the women in question. They would not dare to let such children be born for fear that the husband might abandon them or for fear of a worse fate which might befall them. There were only two girls in the village between the ages of fourteen and sixteen who were about to be turned loose in the Moran villages. They were the central point of attraction in the dance which was held the evening before the lion hunt. They were coy and shy and it seemed to me a pity that these girls were to be sacrificed to so insane a policy which will make them absolutely useless from the standpoint of production of their own kind.

This brings me to the second reason for the extinction of the race; free love among the warrior classes. This is not merely a theory; it is an accomplished fact. In olden times the arrival of a girl baby was not by any means looked upon as a welcome intrusion. If she happened to be one of twins she was killed.

If she was in any way deformed or weakly, the same fate awaited her, hence a scarcity of women. Now, of course, they are all welcome. While formerly every father was looking for warrior sons, now he is satisfied with girls, because the need of sons is no longer felt so keenly. But the fact remains that there are scarcely girls enough to go round. Girls may have lovers, but they must not be partial in the bestowal of their affections on these lovers; girls are community property and they belong to all so long as they are in the Moran kraals. This promiscuity, of course, raises havoc with their maternal proclivities and chance for childbirth. The birth rate in these kraals, I have been told, is practically at the zero point, and that just at the time when the girls should reproduce prolifically because of their excellent physiques. If this question were looked after with a little scientific organization, and if the girls were married off without interference from other men, the women would doubtless become mothers of as fine a race of men as the African jungle can boast. Both men and women are of fine physique and mentally well developed. But, as it is, the chances of regenerating the race are nil. What a fine chance there would be for missionaries to do a work which would immortalize their names not only among the Masai but in the world at large!

The third reason for the decrease in the continuation of the species is the fact that syphilis is rampant among the Masai. I had heard from government officials that the spread of that disease was alarming, but when I came among them it took only the opening of one eye to find out that it was almost universal, especially among the children. No sooner had we arrived in the village than a number of people, especially women, came to us to be treated for their eyes. Among the children there was not one who had healthy optics.

On the first day of my arrival I distributed a quart of solution of boric acid, and I continued this treatment until the end of our stay, when I left them a copious quantity of the same medicine. There was also an alarming prevalence of rashes and sores on the head, which told their own tale. Ulcers and sores on the legs and arms were also plentiful, but they may have been the result of the pernicious habit of wearing those terrible arm bands and leglets, which leave scars beyond description. I cannot say that there were extreme cases such as I have seen elsewhere, but the disease, so far as I could judge, was universal. I understand also that miscarriages are the order of the day, and this is ascribed principally to the spread of this foul disease. Whatever may be the causes of the phenomenon, here is an opportunity such as is not often found for the altruist and the philanthropist to raise himself a monument of lasting glory and utility. To rehabilitate that wonderful tribe of the Masai by a thorough education of these people would mean more than a brilliant star in the diadem of a king or queen.

I am told on good authority that there are at present only twenty thousand Masai left in the country, and this figure is based on the returns of the tax list of the British East African government officials, so that there is little room left for doubt. At the present birth rate it is for this present generation to buckle up or go under, never to be heard of again in the annals of African history of the future. Christianity seems to me the only remedy. The installation of good morals and hygienic principles would be the only salvation for the race. There is a good foundation on which to build a Christian structure, because the people are at heart honest, and their savage desire to kill has already been curbed by the British government. Their moral tendencies as far as sexual relations are concerned would be just as well served through monogamy as it is at present through this absurd promiscuity.

The tradition by which this free love system entered into the tribe hundreds of years ago is so infantile that it would take a convincing talker only a short time to show them the error of their ways. That legend is the old story of all African races that their original forefather had one son and two daughters. They were at war and the son had to take the cattle to a salt lick. One of his sisters went with him, and on various occasions he found tracks of strangers leading up to the kraal which he had built. The next day he took out his cattle and immediately returned to hide himself near the kraal. Then he crept up to the hut, where he overheard his sister making love to an enemy, and he killed the man and went back to the old home to tell his father. Here it was decided that it was better to have the system of free love to preserve peace in the family. It was considered, after this experience, that it was safer to allow the girls to live with the warriors in their kraals where they could make love, sing and dance and be at the same time re-

moved from the temptation of betraying the
stock of their parents.

Formerly when there were raids and wars,
and the warriors were at all times on the warpath or raiding expeditions, there was little
time for excesses of sexual indulgence, but now
that wars and raids have stopped they find
their pastime more in these excesses than in
warlike occupations. Hence the dreadful
menace of being wiped out forever which now
hangs over the tribe.

That there are great difficulties to overcome
I will admit, but they are surmountable. So
far no missionary society has entered on the
field because the Masai are a nomadic tribe and
it would be necessary to follow them from
place to place, which was formerly impossible
owing to lack of roads or traveling facilities.
But now Africa is "Darkest Africa" no longer,
but "Africa lit up." There are passable roads
everywhere, and a missionary equipped with
an automobile would find himself capable of
traveling from kraal to kraal and installing
the principles of common sense and right living, and would be welcomed by both the elders
and the warriors. We were the most welcome
strangers among them, and no sooner had we
arrived than a bullock was killed for the

strangers and the freedom of the kraal was given to us. They were courteous and kind, and when we left they were sincerely sorry.

I had a splendid example of Masai hunting on one of my many excursions from Nairobi to Anguruya's kraal. I was riding across country in a "Hup." The car was headed for a large herd of Kongoni and Grants and a few Zebras.

The Masai guide clicked his tongue and in a low voice said, "Hiko!" ("There!") I looked, as did the chauffeur. I saw a Kongoni, undecided whether to go or stay. Presently the chauffeur (a Eurasian) stopped the car and got out. He walked slowly and cautiously toward the Kongoni. The latter now escaped, but still the chauffeur went on on tiptoe. He was about to make a dash when I saw a baby Kongoni get up and follow its mother. The boy followed, but the fawn left him far in the rear. The boy returned to the car and started her going on the wildest run I ever made in a motor car. He followed the baby Kongoni, which began to run wild in large circles. The Masai guide was alert, watching the proceeding. I tried to stop the mad rush, expecting every minute that the car would be smashed on the big rocks in its path.

But the boy had his Indian blood aroused and took chances which no one but the reckless son of an owner would take.

The baby Kongoni began to tire and emitted a series of short clicks from its choking lungs, sounding very much like the "hoo" of a night owl. It began to turn somersaults, but still kept on. Now the Masai guide opened the door, ready to jump and run after the little fugitive. The man jumped and rolled over twice, brought up against a rock, got up and ran after the little deer. Run! He would have taken the Marathon at any meeting, and coming within reach, he never made an attempt until the little fawn was well within his grasp, and then made one dash for the right hind leg and they rolled over—both baby Kongoni and its captor.

THE MASAI LION HUNT

WHEN I used to give lectures in the U. S. A. on African impressions I always mentioned the Masai as the bravest of all British East African tribes. For illustration, I used to explain how the Masai consider it the greatest sport to surround a lion and to kill it with their spears. Consequently, when I made up my program of pictures for the expedition, I made this one essential point to bring out, if at all possible. Now I am glad to state that I have vindicated my honor as a truthful man and to have actually portrayed in a lasting record that famous lion hunt with spears. I shall here describe this most exciting of all my experiences. But I am sure that my description will fall short of the thrilling chase as it occurred.

In order to make sure of the picture, I secured a lion in captivity who had all the qualifications of the jungle king. He was full grown, with a temper of his own, especially

148

where native Africans were concerned. When, therefore, I came to the Masai country I immediately started out to find out what the natives would do to the lion if I should bring him over there. I met with the greatest encouragement when I mentioned my plans. There were no warriors or Morans in the village where I had pitched my camp, but they were immediately sent for from the Moran village, which was over forty miles away. They had arrived before I had returned from Nairobi with the lion. As soon as they made one another's acquaintance I saw that we were in for a most interesting time. The lion in its cage growled furiously at the Morans, and they, in turn, were so wrought up over this beast, which they instinctively hated, that we had a hard time keeping one Moran from spearing the animal in its cage. This gentleman got so hysterical that they had to take his spear from him and guard him till the moment of the hunt had arrived.

We took great pains in arranging the arena for the coming event. There was a grand spot which had been picked out in my absence. The scene was a flat stretch of dry swamp surrounded by an edge of rushes and tules with a jungle background. The cage was placed between the rushes, facing the flat arena. When all was ready for the operation the Masai warriors ranged themselves around two sides of the circle, which was to seal the lion's fate. It was a veritable Coliseum—only it was reversed in its use. Here the lion was to be the victim and men his executioners. No gun was allowed on the premises. Two American ladies in the party and some other spectators had taken refuge in nearby trees. The two photographers with their machines had taken up their post on a wagon thirty feet from the center of the arena and I joined them with my kodak. The keeper of the lion was to lift the door at a signal given when everything was in readiness for the critical moment.

The Morans were alert, with every muscle and nerve of their splendid bodies taut. The trapdoor rose slowly and creaking. The eyes of the warriors were glued to the figure of the lion, watching his every movement, their spears and shields ready for the attack. The lion appeared unconcerned. He lay down in his cage. I had given orders that under no circumstances must he be molested without giving him a chance to defend himself. We

LION HUNT OF THE MASAI
Warriors arrive at elders village, greet Chief
Dance of victory around the lion's carcass
Queens welcoming lion hunters

LION HUNT OF THE MASAI

Masai warriors at their favorite game of lion hunting with spears

did not wait long before prodding him from the other side, but he refused to enter into the spirit of the moment.

Presently I gave orders to smoke him out, and a fire was lit at the other side of the cage. The smoke turned away from him, and I gave new orders to light one at the front. My orders were not understood, and I had to move over to the cage to have it done. No sooner was a bunch of flaming grass put under his nose than he jumped out of the cage, and coming out in the open, he turned around to measure his chances of escape. There were no Morans in sight at either side of the cage, so he turned to the right and broke cover, leaping up in a bound, and he was off for the chase. We had not reckoned on this eventuality, but the Morans had. They went after him and soon overtook him. He was, however, out of sight of the camera, and quicker than it takes to relate, all of us were after him with cameras and all paraphernalia necessary. The Morans nearest to the beast were ready to seal his fate there and then because he was running toward the village. But fortunately for us, Mr. Klein from New Jersey, who knew the game thoroughly and who spoke the language very well, warned the natives not to use their spears until the camera had come up.

They brought him to bay in a copse surrounding him from two sides. We had the camera trained on him again in short order, and now I gave the Morans the signal to attack. The lion, however, had anticipated my signal by a fraction of a second and charged with a loud roar at the first click of the camera. He crouched on his belly and leapt up in the air, all his savage nature intent on going after the steel monster shining in the brilliant sun. He advanced from one side, the Morans from the other. It was a question who was going to be the first to attack. But the Masai are too old at the game to give the lion a chance. At a distance of twenty feet the first spear was thrown; it missed. The second, following closely, hit the poor animal squarely on the forehead, piercing through the brain and cutting its way clear through till it reached the left shoulder blade. Five more spears were thrown in rapid succession, and all landed, most of them in vital spots. The beast charged directly toward the camera, and when he was struck by the second spear, which killed him almost instantly, he looked dazed, and as it happened, he looked me straight in the eye as if asking, "What did I do to you to deserve this fate?"

The event was so short of duration that it seemed as if it had not been worth all the trouble and expense. But to see the Masai in action was a thing that only few white men have had the privilege of seeing, and a good many of them never lived to tell the tale because their spears are as effective as rifles in the hands of the ordinary "askari."

On this occasion the Morans were wonderful. They are not a muscular race—if anything, they look soft—but they are lithe and wiry, of great endurance and indomitable courage, which, combined with a true sportlike instinct, makes them what they call themselves —an independent, unconquered race. They look you straight in the eye; they do not cringe like other natives. They look stoical. They march up silently, always with spear in hand. When they arrive at a village of elders they shake the hand of the chief, their father, and pass on to the middle of the village, where they await the greeting of the women of the chief's harem. This done, they disperse as if they were dismissed from drill, and each seeks the hut in which he is to be lodged during his stay in the village. In action they are quick and sure of their movements. Fearless, with determination in their eyes, they go to the attack with one aim only—to get the other fellow first. And they usually do. That made them what they are at present, a tribe of unconquered heroes, conscious of the admiration which every white man in Africa has for them.

Before they depart on a military or serious hunting errand the Aigwanian, or leader of their circumcision class, addresses them and lays down the policy to follow. He gives them strategic instructions and orders which no Moran may dare disobey. They listen without a murmur. There is a tone of decision mixed with a complete abandonment to fate in their bearing when they walk toward the scene of the coming battle. Once there, they arrange themselves without a word and await developments. But when the critical moment has arrived they are ready, and it is surprising how much strength is hidden behind their seeming physical weakness. The spears which were thrown at the lion had so much steam behind them that they pierced his body clear through, and it was only with the greatest difficulty that they could be extracted. Two of the spears were bent at an angle of 45 degrees when they had been drawn out of the carcass with almost superhuman efforts. Another spear was broken at the hilt and had to be cut out from where it had lodged.

What makes the Morans especially proud of their achievement on the hunting ground and on the battlefield is the fact that after they have speared an enemy or a lion they are entitled to marry. No Masai girl would look at one until such an event has crowned his military and hunting prowess. Such a victory naturally makes the men supremely happy, and they are willing to lay down their lives for the attempt and a bid for the fair woman's favor. The height of their excitement before the battle is only evidenced by their frantic expressions of joy after the finish. They walk around the carcass, brandishing their spears and holding their shields high up in the air over their heads, and they dance and jump and act like so many maniacs let loose. Only when they are called to order by their Waignanian, or headman, do they fall in line and now they perform a march of victory in an ensemble, the shields still over their heads and the spears straight up like a huge steel bristle, like an ominous warning which must have looked a fearful augury for a routed enemy in bygone days.

It took very little imagination to visualize on that occasion former feats of arms of these Morans, who know no bounds to their conquests. Formerly in battle with their enemies, even if they were outnumbered they would attack again after a defeat until the last man had dropped.

That they do not take any chances was shown by the way they rendered the animal incapable of further harm by severing the spine with a slash of the knife. They made a terrible gash, cutting the spine in two. All this was done in the twinkling of an eye. The whole scene did not take more than a minute. In this case they were fortunate that none of their number had been mauled. Sometimes it happens that the lion is quicker than they are, and one of them is sat upon by the lion before he can get away after throwing his spear. In such a case one of the Morans gets behind the animal and catches him by the tail to divert his attention from the man who is down. They twist the tail and the other warriors assist the first tail-catcher to lift the brute by the hindlegs off the victim. The others then take a thrust at the beast with their spears, or, if he be too dangerous, with a knife or dagger, thus preventing accidents to the surrounding group of fighters.

We all feel very proud and very happy over the successful taking of the picture. This may be better understood when it is known that the attempt to get this picture has been made many a time by different photographers, who never got a foot of film out of their efforts. Mr. Klein of New York, for instance, who witnessed our hunt, told me that he had made nine attempts and every one was unsuccessful. He tried it on three tame lions and on six wild kings of the jungle, but through some accident or other unforeseen event not one picture was taken.

THE WAKAVIRONDO

AFTER we had left the Masai and returned north to Nairobi I was anxious to proceed to the Kavirondo country, which lies about 300 miles west of Nairobi, the capital city of British East Africa. This desire was prompted by various motives. First of all, it was the country where I had suffered most during my missionary career, when I was suffering from acute malaria, half chronic, half intermittent, until finally I had to leave Africa for good in July, 1905. I had always wondered if the game had been worth the candle, and both from correspondence and reports in the annals of the foreign missions I had learned that the work was bearing great and wonderful results.

Secondly, when I first arrived on this expedition at the Port of Mombasa I had visited the Catholic Mission on Sunday morning, and to my great surprise I found a very large congregation gathered around the church on the mission grounds. This was all the more surprising because when I had left Mombasa in 1905 there was an exceedingly small number of Catholic negroes in that mission. Nor did the clergy of this church have great hopes of making headway among the Swahilis, or Coast natives, who were mostly Mohammedans. Imagine, therefore, my surprise when I found some 600 well-dressed natives in and outside that church. I called, therefore, on Father Lutz, the pastor, not only to pay my respects, but to congratulate him on his wonderful success in so difficult a territory. When I mentioned the miraculous transformation of the Swahilis the genial old gentleman smiled and corrected me with a reflective "Tut tut; they are not Swahilis; they are Kavirondos."

It was my turn to be surprised beyond words, and I remonstrated, "Not these people; they are too well dressed and too clean to be Wakavirondo. Besides, they do not show the fallen-in underlips as a result of the missing lower incisors."

"I see you are acquainted with the Wakavirondo," replied the good old missionary.

"I ought to be, considering that I was the first missionary among them in 1904," I answered.

"Then go back among them and look them

over," he said; "although a great number have
all their teeth intact."

I returned without delay to examine them,
and collecting the few words which I remembered of my vocabulary of 2,000 words which
I had composed in 1904-5, I sprung a surprise
among a few groups. They returned my salu-
tations in kind and opened their eyes wide with
wonder how I knew their greetings whilst they
did not remember my face. Presently one fine
stalwart of about 30 years of age jumped out
of a nearby group, and taking my hand and
shaking it wildly and excitedly, asked, "Aren't
you Père Bellagi?"

"That used to be my name in Uganda," I
replied. "And aren't you Ojole's son?"

"Indeed I am," he said in Kiswahili, notic-
ing that I had retained little of the Luo language. Whilst he grinned, I noticed that his
six lower incisors were missing. (This is a
tribal mark of the Wakavirondo. Boys and
girls have them extracted at the age of 10-12,
with a coarse, small iron spike by the medicine
man. The father of the boy keeps both arms
pinioned, and whilst a stick is placed between
the two jaws of the boy, in order to hold his
mouth open, the "dentist" jars out the teeth
with a forcible jerk, the one after the other,

the boy screaming holy murder and bleeding profusely.)

"How is it that you all are so well dressed when last I saw you you even refused to frequent the mission because I insisted on your wearing clothes?"

"Oh, all that is changed in Kisumu, although in the country the Shenzi (pagans) still go naked," he laughed. "There are very many Catholic people there now," which I found later was correct, because there are well over 30,000 of these savages converted and active members of the Catholic Church.

All of this made me impatient to see with "mine own eyes" the reported metamorphosis of this scene of my earlier efforts again. Consequently the three hundred mile ride on the Uganda Railroad was all too slow for me, and I shook myself out of my dusty couch early in the morning, when at 7 A. M. we steamed into the Kisumu railroad yard to get a first glimpse of the old town broiling on the slopes of the Nandi Hills and shimmering in the reflecting rays of a burning sun cast back by the placid expanse of the Victoria Nyanza.

No wonder, then, that the Kavirondo people have always been a great favorite with me for the reason that I started the first mission among them in 1904. And what savages they were then! Well do I remember how I struggled to get them to wear clothes. The terminal station at Kisumu (then called Port Florence) had been established in 1902, and even then, two years later, the men and women used to crowd the platform stark naked. White people were beginning to pour into Uganda and the embarrassing situation which arose when ladies or Sisters arrived was acute.

I well remember how I used to clothe a dozen to fifteen young women every Sunday in the attempt to kill two birds with one stone, showing them the necessity of clothing and the difference of the Sunday and week days. My boy finally stopped me by showing me that the girls went straight from my camp into the market, where they disposed of my cloth for a bit of meat or fish to the Swahili traders, who were the only beneficiaries of my bounty.

Then I tried the government, which was well disposed to me. I asked them to let me clothe 2,000 people and thereafter make a law that no "Omera" should enter the city limits naked. I was referred to Sir Charles Elliott, who was then the Commissioner of the British East African Protectorate. I awaited his arrival and laid the project before him. He scorned the idea, and after a long argument he asked me, as a clinching climax, "Did not Adam and Eve go about the same way in the Garden of Eden?" And I replied that I had always been under the impression that the British government brought civilization wherever they planted the Union Jack, but if he had been sent there to introduce the more primitive customs of the Adam and Eve period I had no more to say, and began to work in my own quiet way. I was there eighteen months, the last eight of which I was so ill that finally I had to evacuate and go home, but the work went on and imagine my surprise.

What struck me as almost remarkable in my researches among the Wakavirondo was the almost miraculous transformation which had converted the natives from the irresponsible, irresponsive, savage and almost animal horde which occupied the eastern quarter of the Victoria Nyanza into a useful and industrious people. In 1904, when I first came upon them, they were a nude and filthy population. They were primitive to the point of eating their food raw. They had no occupation save that of fishing and bartering grains—which they did not grow themselves—for cattle.

The natives wore no clothes, greased their

bodies with a mixture of cow-dung, ashes and butter in order to prevent their skins from cracking in the merciless rays of the sun. And yet the women were not free from the feminine characteristics of their betters in the U. S. A. and Europe; that is, vanity and a great passion for fanciful designs. Only in Kavirondo, having no clothes, silk, velvet or even calico to embroider them on they have them cicatrized or cut into their skins. On the reverse page you will find a good example of such a scarification. The poor vain creature had this artistic pattern cut into the stomach with a crude knife. The upper incisions carved a gash of a quarter inch deep in her flesh, whilst the walls of the incision were turned over with a buttonhook in order to raise the base of the wound to form a "haut relief" ridge as a head ornament of the living escutcheon gradually tapering down till it faded away on the nether abdomen. Such mutilations are very common among the women, whilst the men usually content themselves with slight notches on the face or the breast and shoulders.

They always were a strong and well built race. They were strangers to disease and venereal ravages because, for all their filth, immorality was not one of their shortcomings.

CHECKERBOARD SCARIFICATIONS OF THE NORTHERN
WAKAVIRONDO WOMEN

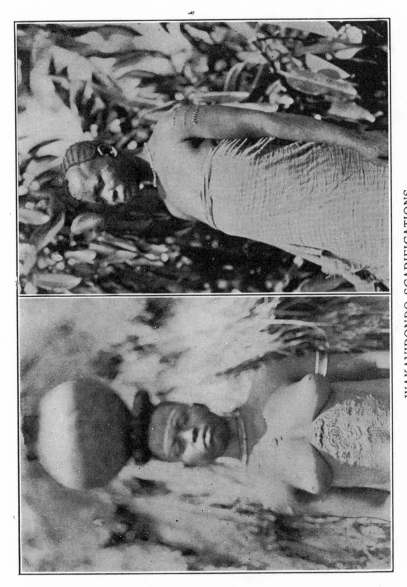

WAKAVIRONDO SCARIFICATIONS

Scarifications of a southern Wakavirondo wom-   Northern Wakavirondo woman of modest scar-

They were moral to a degree unheard of among the surrounding tribes, most of which were dying out as a result of their promiscuity and sexual excesses. The Wakavirondo then, as now, were moral, however we may regard the motives for their code. Whether we ascribe the purity of their young women to a commercial spirit—for they are considered less valuable as matrimonial commodities when they have lost their virginity—or whether we credit them with a refined fundamental morality, the fact remains that they have preserved physical conditions which have assisted them in raising large families of sturdy children.

Physically above the average of Africans on the Equator line, the Wakavirondo are tall, muscular, wiry and capable of unusual feats of endurance.

This quality was well demonstrated during the war, when, according to all critics, they were by far the best porters and did more to conquer German East Africa than any other three tribes combined. At present one may see them scattered along the line from Mombasa to their home in Kavirondo, doing good work as askaries, road builders, mechanics and artisans of every description. They are in great demand on farms and in industrial institutions, for with their docility and desire for learning they are apt pupils in every branch of endeavor. Having learned to clothe themselves, they have abandoned their unsanitary habits and they even wash and bathe wherever they come in contact with Europeans. They stand aloof from the other tribes and consequently do not adopt the evil ways of their neighbors. They are honest, and for that reason they are more popular as servants than any of their competitors from other tribes. They are willing, courteous, and always cheerful, if somewhat reticent; they lack the grasping desire for "baccees" which makes the other natives so objectionable. They are willing "to pay their own way," even where missionary work is concerned, to buy what they wish and even to contribute their mite to institutions from which they derive educational benefits or other cultural advantages.

They are independent by nature, but not aggressive or warlike. Still, they could not be called cowards, and they are able to give a good account of themselves when attacked, without going out of their way to make life unpleasant for their neighbors. Their amiability is so well known that they are called the "Bamera" (our

friends) by the Kakamega, and other neighboring tribes.

The Wakavirondo are not what one might
call a good-looking tribe. On the contrary,
they are unattractive in appearance, owing
chiefly to their ridiculous habit of breaking
out the incisors of the lower jaw. The loss of
six lower teeth makes the under lip fall in and
gives the natives the appearance of prema-
turely aged people. The reason for this habit
coincides with that of other tribes who affect
similar dental vagaries, viz., the wish to be prepared against starvation when attacked by
tetanus.

The Kavirondo call themselves "Luo" and
resent being labeled Kavirondo, whatever that
name may mean. It is supposed by some that
this name was given to them by the Arabs, who
began trading with them in the early fifties.
The same authorities maintain that the name
was derived from the name of Ondo, who was
the ancestor of the tribe. However, the people
themselves have no well-defined idea of their
own origin, and it would be presumption for
any anthropologist to set down a hard and
fast theory of his own and to float it for what
it is worth. The river cannot rise above its

source, nor can scientists or ethnologists go beyond the information obtainable from the natives, who are after all their own historians and more interested in their own traditions than any of us can be. They have no written legends or any tangible historical knowledge of their own; therefore I assert that their own stories, interwoven though they be with innumerable fictions, must be the only authority on which to build a true record of their past.

Their history seems to be as follows: Centuries ago they lived north of their present territory, some claim in the lower Soudan.* Coming down, they migrated in a body and fought

* Since I wrote this article in Kavirondo I pushed farther north and following the Nile I came to a tribe called the Alur, who inhabit the northern part of the Albert Nyanza. They are very similar in physical build and features to the Kavirondo and speak a language almost the same as the Luo language of the Kavirondo natives, from which discovery I would rather conclude that they must be branches of the same race. And since I was informed in that country that the Alur descended from the lower Soudanese territories, it is quite likely that the Kavirondo peoples originated from there. Although I never traveled through the Bakeddi country, I learned from missionaries who resided in that country for years that some of the local tribes in that district are very much like the Alur and the Kavirondo, which would suggest the idea that this exodus from the lower Soudan was split up on various occasions, although it is hard to believe that the Kavirondo should have migrated as far as the western point of the Berkeley Bay or the Victoria Nyanza. And yet, having left the vicinity of large stretches of water such as the Nile base, the Albert Nyanza and the Lake Kyoga, they could be expected to wander southward until they found another large sheet of water such as the northeast arm of the Victoria Nyanza.

their way through the Bantu tribes which they encountered. Their numerical strength overcame all resistance, and the Bantu were unable to make a united stand against them, owing to the fact that they themselves were always engaged in intertribal conflicts. The conquering band of Nilotic adventurers finally settled down on the east border of Lake Victoria, their present home. Why they should have selected their barren and stony location is difficult to understand, considering that they passed through such fine territory as that now occupied by the Nandi and the Washa Ngishu. At any rate, they congregated about Kavirondo, where they split up into numerous clans and sectional groups.

On second thought, I would say that maybe the Nandi and Washa Ngishu plateaux might have been too cold for them, being of so much higher elevation and the fact that they swarmed down from the lower Soudan. Most likely they sought an elevation milder in temperature to that which they had abandoned.

Having settled down in their new territory, they began to breed cattle, in which occupation they were most successful, especially in the region bordering immediately upon the lake. Here the land, rocky and unfit for agriculture, is well adapted for pasturing, and the natives became owners of immense herds of cattle. The land higher up was more fertile and the natives who squatted in that district were able to grow good crops of various grains, which the Luo around the lake bought from them with their cattle. Consequently the Kavirondo are not exclusive meat eaters like some other Nilotic tribes, as, for instance, the Masai or Nandi. Rinderpest and other diseases of cattle decimated the herds time and again, and at the present time their holdings are small compared to what they once were. Now they keep only enough cattle to furnish meat and milk and to use as barter in the purchase of wives.

The Luo, like all other Nilotic tribes, of course, indulge in polygamy on a large scale. A man may have ten, twenty, or even thirty wives, according to his means and temperament. The manner in which a Kavirondo obtains his additional wives and at the same time builds up a village is rather peculiar. A man having married for the first time usually lives in his father's village until the time has come when he is able to set up an establishment of his own. When he has acquired enough head of cattle to treat himself to a few additional spouses he begins to cut down and collect a

AN IMPROVED NATIVE VILLAGE OF A WAKAVIRONDO MISSION

WAKAVIRONDO SAVAGERY
Hut with part of inmates outside
Feminıne curiosity watching the camera
Minstrel in Wakavirondo

certain amount of wooden poles and sticks with
which to build the huts required for the rest
of his harem, in the construction of which he
is assisted by his relatives. A suitable place
is sought as near as possible to his father's
kraal, and the first hut is erected. Gradually
as he collects wives new huts arise successively,
according to an established diagram, which
may be represented as follows:

$$9 \quad 7 \quad 5 \quad 3 \quad 1 \quad 2 \quad 4 \quad 6 \quad 8 \quad 10$$

When he has more than ten wives a new village is erected for the next ten.

Wife A represents the first (1) hut, and
always remains the principal wife, her hut
forming the nucleus of the village. All the
cattle are attached to the first hut, and it is
with these cattle that the husband buys his new
wives. When the first wife has brought forth
her first-born she is thought to need an assistant. Since the second wife is bought with the
cattle attached to wife A's hut and the cattle
buy the wife, wife A, in the Kavirondo law,
buys the second wife and a new hut is built for
wife B at the right of wife A's hut. However, as time goes on, wife A requires more
assistants, and it may be that wife B is in the
same predicament. Wife A therefore buys

still another wife with the cattle attached to her hut and wife C has a hut built on the left side of wife A. When wife B needs help she "buys" another wife—D—with the cattle attached to her own hut, and so the system carries on until a full complement of ten has been obtained. Wife B and wife C are known as the sisters of wife A, and their children form one large family.

Similarly, wife D, paid for by wife B, lives by the side of B in hut 4, and is known as the daughter of B. Near evening the husband sends his chair, which is a sort of milk stool, to the wife whose company he wishes to enjoy during the coming night. This self-invitation is sent out in advance so that the chosen wife may prepare for her lord's entertainment.

Around the village is raised a protective fence made of Euphorbia and in this fence there is only one opening, which is made directly in front of hut number 1. On the inside of this fence the brothers of the husband may build their huts and those of their wives, provided that they have not too many.

The open space in the area of the village is reserved for a cattle pen. The goats, sheep and calves are sheltered in the owner's hut unless they be too numerous, in which case a separate structure is made for them. The pen is surrounded by a fence of sticks and thorn bushes, with a small aperture. This entrance is closed at about 6:30 P. M. Should the owner go out in the evening to attend a sociable drinking bout the entrance is left open just a trifle for his highness.

About 6 A. M. the village gate is opened, and half an hour later the cattle gate is let down. In the meantime the smaller animals have been released from their huts and the calves immediately seek their mothers. The calves are allowed to take their breakfast before the boy attempts to milk the cow. A curious thing about the African cow is that she will not permit herself to be milked until the calf has started the milk flow.

The milk is caught in an earthenware vessel, or sometimes in a scooped-out chunk of wood. These receptacles are cleansed with liquids obtained from the cow; but an account of the production and collection of the fluid involved might be too realistic, for which reason I forbear a more detailed description. Women are not permitted to milk cows, owing to the nudity of the cow. The milk is used to make a gruel for the mutama (a coarse grain), which sometimes is augmented by a slight quantity of blood. This blood is caught at the killing of an animal, and if no animal is killed they follow the method of the Wakamba and bleed the animal—after having pierced its artery with an arrow. The Kavirondo are very skillful at this operation and bleed the bull until he is ready to drop. They repeat the process on the same bull as often as three times a year.

After the milking, the inhabitants of the village repair to their various duties, their herding, their cultivation and their small game hunting. In these villages everybody works but father, and he sits around all day in the "Abila," or rest hut, which is built in the middle of the cattle boma, or near it. Here the elders have their pow-wows and drink their beer. There is another important hut in the village, and that is for boys over six years old. As soon as any of the sons is old enough he builds a hut for himself, and all the boys who have reached six years live with him. At the same age the girls leave their mother's hut and live with their paternal grandmother. I need hardly say that the supervision of the grandmother is rather inadequate, and that it does not prevent the girls from slipping away to spend the night with the boys. Nevertheless, the chastity of the girls is rarely impaired by this practice, but should an offense occur the boy in the case is fined a cow.

In the afternoon at two all return from their work and make preparations for the big meal of the day, which is scheduled for five-thirty. First they fetch water from the lake or from the village waterhole. To see them balance the round jars of water is a sight only found in Kavirondo. First there will be a long line of them, chattering as they go, the leaders gossiping with the vanguard forty yards away and all of them smoking their long-stemmed pipes. All of the village scandal is chewed over on those occasions, because there are no other opportunities for general converse. The water which they draw is beyond description, because the cows drink from the same well, standing knee deep in the water; the children bathe in it; the goats and sheep fight in it, and the water is so putrid and so rank that the mere odor of it would impair a white man's digestion.

The evening milking ends the day of the Luo braves. Their routine is the same day in and day out, and monotonous as it seems, it pleases the natives. It often occurred to me that it is almost a shame to interrupt their happy-go-lucky mode of living with our "modern" European ideas, which create needs and wants of which they formerly were unaware. Sometimes it seems to me as though the introduction of civilization has been detrimental to their happy dispositions and to their one-time complete contentment with life.

They have begun to use every inch of the ground for agriculture and their chief product is mutama, of which there are twenty different varieties. When planting time draws near the young men clear the brush and prepare the soil; the actual tilling and seeding is done by the women and girls. The latter do the weeding whenever necessary, and harvest the crop. The grains mature in four months, and the women cut off the ears one by one and gather them in big baskets. These receptacles are taken to the village and deposited in stationary baskets which look like miniature huts. They are raised three feet above the ground to prevent the rain and ants from spoiling the unthreshed grain. The grain is kept unthreshed, for when it is in this condition a weasel cannot do much harm. A sort of manhole is left near the top of the wall so that the grain may be removed, and sometimes it is necessary to push a boy through the opening to obtain the contents of the hut. These granaries are built of

stalks and twigs and are renovated frequently.
The grain is threshed on a smooth level which
is kept smooth by a copious application of fer-
tilizer. After the threshing of the grain it is
ground by hand on two stones placed in the
veranda in the hut. The stationary grinding-
stone tapers down into a small hole, which is
smoothed on the inside with the usual Kavirondo lubricant. This receptacle is scooped
out again and again, and the flour is collected
in baskets.

The cooking is crude. Culinary operations
are performed in cooking pots which have a
half-inch crust accumulated on the inside from
former preparations which have fermented the
boiling mutama. Stirring with a stick or a
wooden ladle does not improve the combination of the old and new leaven, but the gruel
or mush does not seem to suffer from the infusion of the old crust, judging by the avidity
with which the natives attack it. The real
gourmands make their mutama more tooth-
some by an addition of a gravy drawn from
meat or chicken, which is ladled out into small
dishes. The "bon vivant" takes a lump of
mutama, which he kneads with his fingers and
forms into a little ball, in which he makes a
depression. Then he dips the mouthful in the

gravy dish, filling the little depression, and with resonant gusto the concoction is devoured, although the first tablespoonful would have afflicted a white man with ptomaine poisoning.

The woman who dishes up the food must not walk straight up to the waiting dinner party, but slides in from the side. Nor is she allowed to eat with them, as the Bantu women do. The children also eat by themselves or with their mothers, although kindhearted fathers may occasionally toss them a bone from which the meat has been picked. After the meal has been disposed of the men wash their hands and take a drink of water, the first mouthful of which they spit out and the other of which they keep in their mouths, washing their teeth with their fingers.

Another grain which is commonly grown is the wimbi, a product very similar to canary seed. The wimbi is used principally in the brewing of beer and of other and stronger alcoholic drinks. Some of these beverages are kept standing for a year and make a potion which would set the oldest white toper reeling after the first glass. At present the Kavirondo utilizes every patch of ground which will grow a bunch of grass for their beans, sweet potatoes, pulse, maize and sim-sim, the latter two being produced only for trading purposes. In some parts where the soil is rich they also grow tobacco, but not extensively. This tobacco is allowed to ferment under stones, after which process it is cut. However, most of the tobacco is imported. Formerly only women smoked tobacco, the men preferring hemp, which has the same effect as opium. The British Government has stamped out the hemp habit, and now men also smoke tobacco. Their pipes are made from the same clay used for their pottery and they are baked in small bowls. The stem is made of iron, which is obtained from the Indians. Formerly the pipestems were constructed of reeds. The pipe is passed from friend to friend so that all may get a smoke. The pipe is more or less of a community property, and it is hard to break the natives of this unsatisfactory practice.

The natives of Kavirondo, owing to their traditional antecedents, are naturally fond of fish. The surroundings of their ancestors must have lent themselves to the fish industry, living as they were on the banks of the various branches of the Nile, if not on the border of Rudolf Nyanza. Reference is made in another part of this volume to their probable relationship with the Alur tribe, which occu-

pies the northwestern portion of the Albert
Nyanza and along the Nile, flowing out from
this lake. It may therefore be presumed that
they do not derive their fondness of fish from
strangers.

Most likely proximity to an abundant fish
supply in Berkeley Bay did more than any
other motive to decide their settlement in
Kavirondo. This conclusion seems very plaus-
ible because they have occupied the fringes of
the eastern section of the Victoria Nyanza,
spreading themselves over as long a coast line
as possible, in preference to penetrating deeper
into the mainland.

There is a peculiar interest attached to their
fishing methods, owing to the large scale on
which they operate. Of course, the material
used for this purpose is close at hand and in-
geniously utilized.

Students of Egyptology are aware of the
two principal symbols (the lotus and the
papyrus) found in archeological relics of the
ancient Pharaohs. The extent of the influence
of these ancient autocrats over the lower
Soudan is characterized by the papyrus plant
on all presentations, referring to their power.
And aptly so, because the papyrus is the outstanding feature of the upper Nile. From

QUIET VILLAGE LIFE IN WAKAVIRONDO

An average village.   Village gossipers

Cattle released in the morning.

FISHING INDUSTRY IN WAKAVIRONDO
Weaving the dragnet of papyrus stalks
Weaving the trap of papyrus fibre
The dragnet placed in the Victoria Nyanza

Fashoda up to the Albert and Victoria Nyanza the stately papyrus stalk is ubiquitous, bowing its gracefully plumed head with an alluring welcome which has tempted many a white intruder to an early grave with its deadly breath hidden in a limitless ocean of Sud. The Nile is not so treacherous to its own native sons; on the contrary, the ever-ready papyrus stalk, as the native product of the Nile, furnishes the network, baskets and drive mesh of their fisheries. It is not merely an industry, but partly a sport of which the Luo are very fond. They prepare their nets with consummate skill and admirable patience. Large bundles of papyrus stalks are collected and strung on a vertical line of the same material, taking great care to twist the plumes below the waterline of the drive net. This net is too bulky and heavy to drag. For this reason they manufacture cone-shaped traps, which are inserted in the net at intervals of from twenty to thirty feet. Drivers encircle the base of the net around a semicircular line in boats and floats, driving the fish in the direction of the net. The fish, finding their flight cut off, follow the net, which looks more like a submerged papyrus fence than a net, and seek safety in the large openings of the traps, in which they

are caught and slowly gathered in to shore.
The great bulk of the fish is dried and smoked
for the market of Usoga, Uganda and other
parts of the interior.

Prohibition has not yet been suggested to
the Luo, and I wonder how they would receive
it. Why should they worry about it so long as
their beer is not up to the 2.75 mark? Although they indulge frequently and copiously,
they cannot be accused of drunkenness or of
great excesses. Their beer contains little alcohol, and is more of a food than an intoxicant.
It is made from the unground mutama, which
is poured into a large urn of water. The grain
is allowed to ferment for a day, and in order
to promote the process they add a few ashes
from the fireplace. The following morning
the grain is skimmed from the urn and put in
a basket, which is tied up with leaves. Here
it remains for three days to allow the fermen-
tation to continue until the grain becomes very
soft. A papyrus mat is then spread on the
floor and the grain is put out to dry so that it
may be ground. The ground grain or flour is
now boiled, and it is stirred continuously, so
that it will not burn. Now it is ready for the
filter, which is a large sack of grass. For a
second time it is boiled, and when the mixture

has reached the boiling point the beer is ready for use. Needless to say, the beer is not bottled or drunk out of glasses, but the urn, or "nsuwa," is placed in the middle of the hut and the guests array themselves about it and imbibe through a long reed. The reeds are passed round, and when the beer is about to be exhausted, they add more boiling water.

There is another kind of beer made of canary seed which contains more alcohol and keeps longer. This they store and use for the great occasions, such as births, marriages, funerals and other state ceremonies.

Their economic and judiciary system is somewhat patriarchal. The whole family grows up together and settles down around the paternal home. All their cattle are herded together, and all property, such as cattle, flocks and personal belongings, are communal. The older men and elders used to settle all differences whenever and wherever they might arise. The British Government has changed the mode of procedure by appointing certain chiefs, to whom they have given large districts as their spheres of jurisdiction. These chiefs are assisted by overseers.

This system, however, is not satisfactory, because many of these leaders do not belong to what might be called the nobility or elite of the tribe. It is the duty of the chiefs and overseers in concert to settle all native disputes concerning the ownership of women, cattle, land and other matters. In case no decision can be reached the action is appealed to the higher court of white men—the government officials of the district. When a fine is imposed in such cases the money goes to the treasury as part of the public revenue. Bribery, of course, exists on an extensive scale among the natives.

The Wakavirondo have no modified statutes or laws, but they have an unwritten law derived from traditions and customs "to which the memory of man runneth not to the contrary." For instance, to have killed a man in a quarrel is a great honor; to steal a cow or something more valuable is deemed a clever performance if "you can get away with it." Adultery, in the strict sense of the word, is punished very severely, and rape or seduction may be the cause of intertribal warfare. A man apprehended in an act of bestiality practically becomes an outcast, and one who commits suicide is buried outside the village as a token of utter disgrace. At one time suicide among women was quite common.

Wakavirondo marriages are exogamous. They must not marry within the same clan or within a certain degree of relationship. As with all Africans, obtaining a wife is a question of barter and sale. The price paid for a woman in the Luo tribes is from ten to fifteen head of cattle and the bride is not consulted in the transaction. However, the full price is not paid at the beginning of the marriage rites. As exogamy is strictly enforced, a man must seek out a girl in a village far distant from his own. Before the arrival of the Europeans it was not safe to venture far from home into unknown villages, and the custom arose which made a wife-hunter go to the village of a friend to look over the local marriage market. If the fastidious young man was not suited, his friend took him to a more distant village, and so the suitor proceeded on an almost endless chain until he found an acceptable candidate.

Having been accepted by the fortunate young woman, he would go to her father or eldest brother and make formal application for her hand. His friends, who accompanied him on his quest, also went with him to the parents of the girl. The financial details settled, the girl left her people with the bridegroom after she had taken off her fringes (the

only garment she wore) and accompanied him
without a stitch of clothing.

Toward evening her sisters and other female
relations set out after her, singing to the accompaniment of the harp. When they reached
the bridegroom's temporary dwelling place
they entered and spread a hide on the floor,
placing the bride upon the skin. The boys
then put the bridegroom down the same way
and all left the hut with the exception of two
girls and two boys, who remained to witness the
consummation of the marriage. At the conclusion of the ceremony the four young people
gave a signal by raising their voices loudly, and
the guests outside sang the praises of the young
couple, who were now solemnly betrothed.
The next morning the female relations of the
bride went home and on entering the village
strew ashes on the heads of the bride's parents
as a symbol of sorrow at the departure of the
girl. The mother gave the girls a meal of sim-
sim and presented them with some mutama,
from which they prepared a delicious broth.
With the fat which they had received the girls
smeared their bodies.

In the meantime the bride, who has stayed
with the bridegroom, has been presented by
him with a tassel made of the core of papyrus.

This she fastens on a sort of belt and lets it dangle from her back instead of in front, as she wore the fringes before she was married. Her only clothes before marriage are her fringes, which are six inches long and two inches wide, and after marriage her costume is confined to the plume of papyrus fiber about five inches long dangling from the back. Another gift from the bridegroom is a little piece of iron, well polished, which the bride hangs from her waist only during her bridal days. (She is only a bride and is not called "wife" until the day when she begins to cook for her husband.) After ten days the father of the bride prepares a banquet of goat meat, which the boy and girl friends take to the newlyweds; the boys carry the uncooked legs, the girls bring the balance of the meat cooked. Old women who may wish to join in the feast must bring the drinks. This feast is called "Myasi."

After this first feast the girls are joined by the bride's mother to take the bride home. Here the father prepares another feast, to which the villagers contribute their modicum in the form of boiled meat, and all partake. When the mother returns the bridegroom sends two of his boy friends with an animal to the father-in-law as the first installment of the marriage price. Hereafter the bride doffs both the tassel and the fringes and goes about nude until it is time to go permanently to her husband.

The bridegroom now presents a goat to the bride's sister, who has fixed a tassel for the bride. If he overlooks this ceremony he will be punished at his death by the wailing of all the women, wearing their tassels as a sign of contempt.

When the greater part of the dowry has been paid the bridegroom kills a bull and carries the legs, ribs and half the breast to the bride's relations, who convey the offering to the father of the bride. The remainder of the meat is consumed by the bridegroom, neighbors and relations.

From now on the bride lives with her husband and begins to cook for him, as well as doing her housewifely duties. Only once more does she leave him, and this time he offers another cow to her mother. Thereupon she returns and settles down.

There is one ceremony of a very impressive nature which the bride's father performs before the girl leaves him for all time. He takes a quail and makes an incision in its beak. He ties the quail around her neck with a string provided with some shells. He kills a goat to provide a parting feast, and the girl, bedecked with quail and shells, goes back to her husband for better or for worse.

Another ceremony worthy of note occurs three or four years after marriage, when the bridegroom is called upon to kill a bull in honor of his father-in-law. He notifies all his friends and they accompany him to join in the feast. They drive the bull before them and follow in small groups. Arriving at the father-in-law's village, they adjourn to the banquet and sing extravagant praises of the bride and bridegroom. They paint and grease their bodies fantastically and make the night merry with their dancing and singing. This ceremony is called "Kiscra," and the "morning after" all disperse.

These ceremonies are observed for every marriage regardless of how many wives a man may have.

Divorce is very common among the Luo. When a man sends his wife away, or when she leaves him, however slight the provocation, all of his cattle are returned. The restitution may be a prolonged process, because frequently the brothers of the bride have used the cattle to purchase wives. The children of the marriage belong to the father. One or two heads of cattle are left as remuneration for the relatives of the wife.

Apart from marriage there are certain occasions on which, according to Kavirondo custom, the girls may make love to the boys without contracting or promising any further relation of marriage or serious attachment. However, it is the opinion of the best authorities that there is no actual conjugal relationship or its equivalent going on during such séances.

The fun is conducted in the following manner: The girls, prettily oiled and arrayed in their Sunday best—a new tassel and fringes—proceed to a district where one of their relations lives. Here they are met by the boys, who likewise are greased and painted picturesquely. Upon accosting one another they shake hands, a process which, according to their custom, consists of a series of hand gymnastics. Following this introduction the girls retire a few paces and begin to sing and dance the praises and the attractive features of the boys. The boys in turn retire and sing and dance, repeating their evolutions constantly. Presently both sides dance in concert, and slowly but surely they sidle up to one another. When a boy finally has decided upon a certain

girl he approaches her and taps her gently
on the head with his club. If the girl is agreeable the young couple retire from the crowd
and make arrangements to spend the night together. The dance continues until all of the
boys and all of the girls have mated off. Of
course, the consequences of these adventures
are not serious and lovemaking is merely a
form of polite diversion. The girls stay with
the boys for about three days, after which they
return home.

There is another way of making love. He
and she will have a long talk together, and if
his sentiment is reciprocated they will agree
to marry. The boy then takes a blade of grass
and the girl breaks it as a pledge. This is
called "Muma." Should either party be un-
faithful to this pledge he or she will have evil
fortune in later life, and to prevent this catastrophe the girl's father and the father of the
boy, mellowed by a social drink, will arrange
for the marriage of their children. Frequently
such a marriage is a failure, because the young
couple arranged it only on an impulse and
later went through with the ceremony so that
no disaster would overtake them. In this instance, when the boy and the girl do not marry
officially they may live together with the "ben-

efit of clergy." Elopements are rare, and when they occur the parents of the girl try to recover their daughter. Should they fail, they try vigorously to extort a few heads of cattle from the male eloper's family in payment of a dowry.

It sometimes happens that a man or a boy induces a married woman to leave her husband and marry the interloper. In this case the first husband generally bewitches his wandering spouse by taking something which belonged to her, such as a lock of hair, a piece of fingernail, a rag or some other article which has come in contact with her, and hangs it up in a large oval-shaped calabash. So long as this spell is continued she will never thrive, and as a rule such women waste away until they are dead. To prevent her death she often consults a witch doctor, who sacrifices a goat, the entrails of which he examines while mumbling some prayers, and after this he will produce the article which the first husband has suspended in his hut. The spell, however, is so potent that in one authentic case where the husband's talisman was actually identified by the guilty woman she never recovered, and died a few days later.

The birth of a child is anticipated with the

BLACKSMITHS IN WAKAVIRONDO

Working under handicap of leaking bellows made of joined goatskins.

HOUSEBUILDING

Many hands make light work of the building of a new church in Wakavirondo

greatest anxiety both by the father and mother, the former hoping it will be a boy and the latter praying that it will be a girl. A barren woman is despised among the Luo, and not infrequently a marriage contract is broken off when it is found that the woman will be childless.

The Wakavirondo reckon ten lunar months from the time of conception to the date of birth and on that great day a woman too old to bear children is called in to nurse the prospective mother. If the baby is a boy he is washed by his grandmother and by the midwife. The cold water used for this initial ablution is poured into an earthenware pot and an ax is put in the pot to signify that the boy will help his father in the building of huts. There is no such ceremony for a girl. Before a woman has borne a child or if she has borne only girls to her husband no ax is allowed inside the hut because the wife has not given her husband an assistant builder. The ax is left outside the house, or in the granary until the first male child is born.

Immediately after the child is born it receives a name which as a rule is decided upon as a result of some dreams which the father or mother had had during the time of pregnancy.

If there has been no dream the witch doctor is called in to name the child. He consults the pebbles and the calabash, which he shakes and rattles until the name is revealed to him. Usually he finds the name of an ancestor and tells the parents to call the child by that name. For this service he receives a basket of mutama. If the woman is a second or later wife, she receives from her mother (we must recall that the Wakavirondo refer to the first wife as the sister or mother of the others) a razor with which to shave the head of the baby after four days. The father's head is also shaved with this implement. This razor is kept religiously in a calabash. If the baby is a boy two horse beans are fastened between the legs of the child to notify the world at large that he is a boy, after the naming and shaving ceremonies. When the baby is a girl a string made of the core of papyrus is tied around her waist to proclaim her sex.

The names of the new-born Luo formerly were designed to indicate certain events during which the child was born. For instance, the prefix "O" was attached to the name of the event for the boy and the prefix "A" for a girl. Hence Olwenyo was the name of a boy born in war-time, Lwenyo meaning war, and Ayo was the name of a girl born on the road, Yo meaning road; Otieno was a boy born in the night—and so on.

When a woman is barren the witch doctor is consulted, and he orders the sacrifice of a goat, a chicken or a cow. The chosen animal must be sheltered in the same hut with the woman. If a goat has been selected the top of his ear is cut off and a hole is pierced through the fragment, which the poor woman must carry suspended from her neck. If a chicken is chosen the center claw is cut off and worn similarly. The cow is not touched. The animal must never be killed, and when the goat grows too old one of its kids is substituted. This remarkable fetish is kept up for years, and through generations, so that, even when the first cause of the sacrifice has passed, the relatives of the woman still continue the practice.

Twins are despised, and when a pair is born the parents must stay in the hut for at least a month, never going out even for the most necessary human needs. The first of the twins is called Apigo and the second Agongo irrespective of their sex. The songs which are sung on this occasion are not fit to be heard nor even recorded. The father, the mother and even the other children if there are any, tie leaves of morning glory on their backs above their waists and all the time drums are beaten.

At the end of the month the ashes and dirt accumulated in the house are put on the veranda outside and the hut is ready to be reopened. When the inhabitants have emerged they immediately prepare a great feast to which their neighbors and friends are invited. The guests bring presents of food, drink, wine and beads. Beer is brewed in great quantities and at night the dance of the twins is performed. This dance is so orgiastic that even among the pagans the boys and girls are not permitted to witness the display. However, the dance settles the fate of the twins. The dirt and ashes which have been taken out of the hut are now covered over, the supposition being that all who step on the refuse will rot away slowly. After these ceremonies there can be no more twins in the family.

A similar ceremony takes place when a woman who has been suffering from certain irregularities conceives. When the child is born the parents are again shut in their hut but for a shorter period of time. The same ceremony is followed although not on so elaborate a scale as when twins are born. Nevertheless, here is another occasion for the exchange of presents and for a drinking and dancing bout.

Kavirondo is noted for the strange and uncanny rites which mark the burial services of the dead members of the tribe. Wailing occurs in all the tribes as a manifestation of sorrow but owing to the close proximity of the villages Kavirondo is a nuisance for a white man to live in owing to the fact that there seems to be a wake all the year round. The long cadences of the wailing dirge are particularly annoying and disturbing at night especially since they are accompanied by a monotonous muffled sound of drums. What made me investigate in a detailed manner into these funeral rites was a discovery I made of a gruesome custom in Mumias.

It was a sultry day when I started out for Mumias, hot and suffocating. In the morning we had a little excitement in the form of a Vimy Vichy aeroplane sailing into Kisumu where the natives, no longer astonished at anything the white man might do, took the aerial monster for a big bird (ndegge) and promptly proceeded to dance around it as if it were a festival occasion for which they had been waiting for a long time. It was not only the first aeroplane which had come into that part of the country, but the first one to make an attempt to cross the African continent from north to south or from Cairo to the Cape.

Leaving the big monster to the admiration of the Kavirondo I started west on this long hot trip to get some routine customs of the tribe but what was my surprise when I found one of the best records awaiting me at the other side. We had a barrel of trouble but it was worth all that and more. My chauffeur even was arrested for ignoring the commands of His Majesty, a snobbish young English police sergeant. But even that was forgotten and contributed to the arrogant ambition of John Bull's surplusage of his aristocratic poor relations. What we got was an excellent record of the Kavirondo method of burying their dead in a sitting position with the head left above the ground.

The death and burial of a Kavirondo differs completely from that in any other tribe with which I am acquainted. When the death of a native is expected he is put on the bare floor. All of his clothes, if he possessed any, are taken from him, he is stripped of his ornaments and he is left alone to fight his last struggle with

A WAKAVIRONDO VILLAGE CHIEF
Sugar loaf hat is his distinctive headgear.

WAKAVIRONDO WARRIORS IN FULL WAR PAINT READY FOR THE FUNERAL

death. The Kavirondo are careful to deprive
him of his ornaments for fear that the evil
spirit will haunt his relatives and friends and
that the victim himself never will have peace
after the fatal hour. His last breath is not allowed to escape him before his relatives begin
to push his legs up against his chin, and fold
his arms, with the hands upward. As soon as
he has breathed his last, the women and girls of
the village begin the death wail, which can be
heard far away; the dead man's warbonnet is
hoisted up on a flagpole placed near his hut.

At this signal the neighboring boys prepare
for the funeral rites, and early the next morning they journey to the next village where the
dead man lived. They drive the cattle out to
graze for themselves, while they paint themselves for the occasion. The boys put on full
war costumes with spears in hand and head
gear to crown their nakedness. The hats are
monstrous apparitions, and ought to rouse the
dead from their graves. They are large
sugar-loaf-shaped creations, covered with a
monkey skin or ostrich feathers and with
ostrich plumes jabbed into them from all sides.
If no crown is available the boys stick feathers
all over their hair, which fashion makes them
appear fantastically absurd. From their arms

they suspend the ends of cow tails, which are allowed to trail along the ground. They fasten fetlocks made of strips of skin around their ankles. Their heads are smeared with a reddish clay or with greased ashes, which give them a ghastly appearance and their faces are covered with a paint of various ochers, which gives them a fearfully war-like appearance.

Formerly on the death of a prominent man they used to make a raid on some neighboring village whose inhabitants were supposed to have brought down on them this calamity. Now they roam about the countryside until eleven o'clock in the morning when they arrive at the village where the death occurred.

On hearing the horns of the boys the women increase their wailing and some of the boys now enter the hut and carry the corpse, depositing it outside the hut near the entrance. The mourners on their arrival join in the chorus of lamentation, and even the cattle seem to take up the strain by lowing. Indeed, the noise is maddening. The boys finally squat down on the ground and the burial takes place, the grave having been dug. If the father, mother or oldest child dies, the grave is dug inside the hut, but the younger children are buried outside the house under the veranda. Sometimes when an old and revered inhabitant has died, the natives build a new hut as a mausoleum to rest in. The wife, assisted by some women and one man, digs the grave for her dead husband, and the husband, assisted by some women, does the same for his deceased wife. Young boys help the father to bury the son, and young girls and the mother lay away the daughter. The grave is patterned somewhat in the shape of a box, narrow at the feet and broadening out at the shoulders. The head rests on a cushion formed of earth, and in many cases it is laid in a sort of alcove, dug away from the main grave. A man's head rests on his right arm, and the woman's is placed on the left of her body.

The relations who live in the village where the person has died do not cook their food or milk their cows for three days, but receive their food and milk from friends who sympathize with the bereaved. The first evening after the death they kill a sheep to pacify the spirit of the departed. The skin of the sheep is cut into small strips which the girls and children tie around their wrists and ankles, while the boys make rings for their little fingers. After the dead person has been in his grave for three days, the house is swept and all the villagers walk up the path leading to the house, and are shaved. When the father dies the oldest son is put on the father's chair, and some article used by his parent as a hoe, a stick, or a pipe is given to the son to signify that he is the legal heir and successor.

The ceremonies have now begun in real earnest and presently the boys and the men, decked out in full war paraphernalia riding on or walking behind their pet cows, begin to gather. The women and girls also come up slowly in their invisible costumes, greased liberally, all of them anxious to join in the funeral service. All walk together to the house where the burial is taking place and in procession they march to a large open space, where they give vent to their feelings of sorrow in the most violent manner. It looks more like a tournament than a funeral service. The men and boys array themselves in two lines, and run up and down furiously, until finally they begin to charge at one another as in battle. When they come together the clash does not materialize, they stick their spears in the ground with a flourish, and draw them out to return to a new charge. This sham battle continues for a long time until the women's turn has come. When the sign is given, women and girls raise a most unearthly howl, beating the air and stamping their feet on the ground like a mob of maniacs. They continue their efforts for three-quarters of an hour, after which they are completely exhausted. At three o'clock in the afternoon they retire and go home. If the deceased is a person of importance this service will be repeated after a few months.

A woman bewails her husband for two or three months and her child for one month. The men and boys finish their mourning in a few days. If death takes too large a toll the Kavirondo abandon their village and build elsewhere because the evil spirits have gotten control of the place. In this case they pile stones on the graves so that other people will not cultivate the ground. They revere the dead, and offer up many sacrifices for them in order to pacify their spirits which are supposed to roam about. Suicides, many of whom are women, used to be buried outside the village and a sheep was killed and offered as a sacrifice by throwing a small portion of its flesh toward the sun. They scourged the tree on which the suicide had hung himself with the entrails of a sheep, after which they dug up the tree with all its roots; it was then left so that it could be easily burned. If a person hanged himself in the house, the same sacrifice of the sheep was performed, and the sheep skin cut into strips which the women wore around their necks. The body was buried under the veranda, and the house abandoned and shunned until it fell down and only then was another one built.

I mentioned above that I found practised in Mumias (the northwest corner of the Kavirondo district) a custom of burying the body of a dead chief with the head protruding above the ground. Of this I saw an example of a chief (the brother of the famous Mumia) who had died in September, 1917. The details of the custom call for the evacuation of the hut in which he died by everybody except his two favorite wives. The latter guard the remains in the hut where he is buried with his head above the ground. This head or skull they grease with butter daily until the fleshy substance has disappeared. During all this time they cover the head with an earthenware cooking pot after the dressing. When finally the bare bony skull only remains the head is wrenched from the vertebræ and buried with the balance of the remains. About that time the hut also falls into ruins and the two widows

ENJOYING NATURE DRINKS
Light refreshment during the dance
Two topers enjoying their home brew

SAVAGE ENTERTAINERS

Ukamba jester. He is not as silly as he looks   Wakavirondo saxophone made of gourds
                                                  Wakavirondo warrior in full war paint

have another hut or two built close by where
they live out the balance of their days dutifully
guarding the spot where once the "Master"
lived.

A murderer used to be considered a hero and
honored as such. When a group of men had
killed an enemy clansman the murderers would
go to the nearest village having painted their
right cheeks with a reddish ocher and their left
with a whitish—a confession of the crime. A
male sheep was killed and the skin was cut into
long strips which the murderers wore suspended from their arms. In the meantime
some charms composed of certain woods were
collected and sprinkled over the neighboring
villages as though a blessing were being im-
parted. If a murderer had not blessed the
village and he met a person of that village the
person he encountered would die.

Formerly when a murder was committed by
a single party the murderer received in each
village which he entered a chicken or another gift of similar value. A day or two
after a murder all went to the village where the
murder had been committed and sang the
praises of the murderer. After four days the
villagers used to go to the river to wash themselves, threw strips of sheep skin into the river,

and suspended from their necks owls whose beaks had been cut. Now murderers go to the paths leading to the market from the villages and receive the offerings of men and women going to the market. These offerings consist of grain, flour, meats, and the like. A murder was often followed by tribal and clan wars, but for this reason the British government has lately managed to stamp out most of the incentives to this crime.

THE CONGO

HAVING completed our work in Kavirondo our party took the *S. S. Winifred* to Ntebbe, the governmental headquarters of Uganda. On the Victoria Nyanza many memories crowded each other into the background as we sailed along smoothly on the mirrorlike surface of this Mid-African lake on which not a ripple broke the brilliant sheet of reflected sunlight.

My first voyage on the little *Ruwenzori* came vividly before my revision of the past when, in 1897, I had skipped from island to island and occasionally to a banana plantation on the mainland to seek for night shelter or food. When the Bavuma Islands hove into sight I remembered the times when I had been rowed from the borders of Kyagwe in native canoes manned by a dozen or more strong muscled oarsmen, whose rhythmic strokes, accompanied by monotonous if loud songs of spontaneous composition, moved the frail shivering excuse for a boat with marvelous speed towards their fishing hamlets.

The sight of the now deserted Kome Islands recalled the deplorable ravages of sleeping sickness which, in less than two years, had laid waste a thickly populated group of thriving fishermen's communities, leaving only sad memories to the missionaries whose efforts had built up such promising missions. I could almost feel the graveyard silence which hovered over the fertile and luxurious wilderness of their dark green forests, bleeding with nature's own abundant rubber supply. The sad memories of the hundreds of natives whom I had silently witnessed sleeping their lives away into unconscious extinction almost seared my soul. I could see my old friend Mumbo even now standing before me with his jubilant court, when he announced his elevation to the chieftainship of these Kome Islands, which he only governed a couple of years before the great catastrophe spread its sure but silent talons over the little archipelago to crush out every living soul of its prosperous units.

Skipping away from this group of islands, I glued my glasses on the next, comprising the Sesse Islands which, although I had never visited them, yet will always bring back to me

the poor misguided rivalry between the French
Catholic and English Protestant missionaries
of the late eighties and early nineties, when
finally a long brooding spirit of jealousy
culminated in the fierce war of the Bangereza
and Bafaraza (English and French); when
Bishop Hirth had been fired upon by Captain
Williams when he escaped with King Mwanga
of Uganda across this very sheet of water
which I now traversed. And yet again this
very rivalry had worked its own way to make
the native partisans loyal to the cause they had
espoused and made them use all their influence
on their friends, which precipitated the almost
general choice of religion in Uganda so that
this central tribe in Africa may now be classed
as a Christian tribe amid the surrounding riot
of paganism.

Crossing from port to starboard, I now
gazed on the well known hills of Uganda,
among which my happiest years were spent.
My very soul was stirring when I recognized
Nakasero's long straight sky line around
whose sloping curves I crawled on that never-
to-be-forgotten September night in '97 when
I had been recalled from my inland mission
to join the slender European forces against the
700 well armed Soudanese mutineers. Con-

flicting native reports had it that the mutineers
had surrounded Kampala from the Northeast
and strung a chain of outposts across my
path leading into the capitol, and guided
by a Muganda Mussu hunter I had been
led silently through the high elephant-grass-
covered mitala into Kampala, only to find out
that the mutineers were held on the other side
of the Nile.   But that night and the succeed-
ing ten days of suspense and the long guerilla
war following, when 700 guns and practically
all available ammunition were in the hands of
the Nubians and we were cut off from all assistance by more than a thousand miles, when
there were only 40 whites in the whole Protectorate; those long night vigils in solitary posts
where silent hostile scouts crouching toward
the white centrals were forever on search for
one's life like leopards of the dark; when one
only could rely upon the bravest and most
faithful of one's mission boys and all others
had fled to safety; when Nanganga had surrounded me three times at night and I was at
his mercy, having not one gun on the premises,
and he, the old elephant hunter, supported
with 40 rifles, and I had outmaneuvered him by
having the war drums beaten with scarcely a
dozen unarmed boys around me; all these remi-

niscences passed my memory as in a parade of black ogres. But amidst them rose my Baganda friends, whom I was now about to visit again after an absence of 17 years.

Having landed at Ntebbe, an agent of Childs and Joseph, a New York firm, whisked me now in a motor car to Kampala on splendid roads where, on the night of 13th May, 1897, Father Biermans (now Bishop of Uganda) had led me by the hand through narrow footpaths when I was blind from the effects of the tick fever and together, strangers in a strange land guided by a mission boy, we arrived unannounced at the reed gate of the Nsambya mission at 2 A. M. after traveling six months and seven days from London to this our destination. "Mengo of the Seven Hills" came into view and with it my seven years of hard service and successful efforts shot into the retina of my eyes like a vivid living picture as I had seen them only in my dreams and disstant contemplations during this long period of absence. What blissful memories surged into my very being physically shaking my frame with their absorbing thrills such as only pioneers may lay claim to!

I wish I had time and space here to set down the pleasant experiences of the next four weeks in Uganda, but I must leave them for another chapter or maybe a book on the Baganda whom I must now only mention "en passant" and in transit to the Congo.

Leaving Uganda we wended our way part by road and part by steamer to Jinja, the source of the Nile in Usoga. Here we followed the Nile as far as the lake Kyoga which we crossed on a comfortable flat-bottom steamboat. It is worth mentioning here as a digression that the Nile is 3,461 miles long whilst the elevation of Jinja is 3,462 feet, leaving the Nile a fall of one foot per mile on its long journey to Alexandria on the Mediterranean.

There are two features in the illustrations of this collection which are foreign to the contents of the book, but the pictures are too rare to cast them aside, and a little explanation will be necessary to elucidate their meaning.

The hippopotamus picture was taken by Mr. Klein, who killed it. The name of the "horse of the Nile" which really belongs to the pig family rather than to the equine genus, is a mistaken nomenclature for which the early philologicians are more to blame than the biologists. The Nile is teeming with them, and we saw schools of 50 and 60 of the beasts from

A "HIPPO" IS A GIFT OF THE NILE
Light spot showing hippo coming up for a breath
The carcass is rolled up the bank
Saffari boys enjoying the leatherlike meat

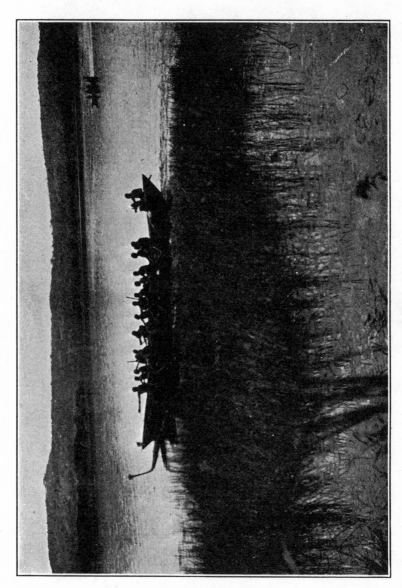

CANOE RACING

At the source of the Nile near Jinja

the railing of the *Caisar*, which took us from Rajaff to Karthum.

The porters of a caravan are very fond of "hippo" meat, although it is altogether too tough a task for our white digestions to tackle.

The Shilluck are a Nilotic tribe who live on the west bank of the Nile in and around Fashoda, of Colonel Marchant fame. Whilst the Pigmies in the Congo Forest are the smallest race in Africa, so are the Shilluck the tallest. Of the hundred and more Shilluck I saw there were at least four who measured over 7 feet, whilst there was not one under 6 feet.

The men have a peculiar mode of hair-dressing. They spread out the hair on the crown or tonsure in the form of a matted flat surface very similar to our collegiate caps. The impression of this fanciful design topping an otherwise totally naked appearance looks very ridiculous. The Shilluck are fearsome warriors with long shields made of crocodile hides and long spears which at rest are planted in the ground, head down. Their dance is more like a warlike attack than a "gyratic" performance.

After crossing the Kyoga Lake on another flat-bottom stern-wheeler we landed at Port Masindi in Bunyoro, where we started on another cross-country jaunt, part by motor truck and part on foot, to Butyaba on the east coast of the Albert Nyanza.

The Congo had always been an alluring mystery to me. Now we were so near that I could not withstand the spell of the forest and I decided to lift that enigmatic veil which had always hung over this far-famed wilderness. The Pigmies particularly were fairytale phantoms whom I longed to see in the flesh, however far they might be removed from the public eye. Their elusiveness seemed to grow in reverse proportion to our distance from them, and this only whetted my appetite.

We had been through Uganda and Busoga, and since I had planned to go back by the Nile route, we made arrangements to include a visit to the Pigmies. The most peculiar thing about the route to the Congo is that no one in British East Africa seems to know much about it, and I had given up trying to find out anything definite as to time tables or the direction in which we had to travel. I discovered in Uganda that there were two routes open, the Kasenyi and the Mahagi entrée. These two ports on the western shore of the Lake Albert were the only certain guideposts of which we could learn. As to plans for further traveling

or data concerning the shortest routes to the
Pigmies, there were so many different opinions
—mostly supported by hearsay only—that I
made up my mind to trust in chance.

Therefore I sent half of our party on to
Nimuli to finish whatever exposed film had not
been developed, and Dr. Shattuck and I
stepped ashore at Mahagi Port the day after
we landed in Butyaba. I had tried to get
transportation to Kasenyi, which is the south-
most port on the Albert, by rowboat or sailing
vessel, but the commander of the ports raised
all sorts of objections on account of the rough-
ness of the lake. I remonstrated that the dangers were ours, not his, but this made the old
seadog all the more stubborn. I then tried the
Provincial Commissioner, who I was told,
might secure me a native canoe with enough
rowers to get us to the Congo from Butyaba
in three days.

Here I struck a new objection—that of the
sleeping sickness, which is still raging along
the shore of the Albert Nyanza. A number of
formalities would have to be gone through
which would take more time than we could
save by taking the southern route. So at the
eleventh hour we decided to go to Mahagi, the
port of call of that week, and had to add an-

other two weeks to our already long trip through these inhospitable regions. I had hoped that we might be able to get down from Mahagi to the Forest and back again in time to catch the next week's steamer from Kasenyi back to Butyaba and Nimuli, but little did I then know what problems confronted us.

No sooner had we reached Mahagi than the plot began to thicken. We seemed fortunate in meeting two Belgian Government officials who had been in the country for a long time and who, I supposed, would be better able than any one to give us definite information. Nothing was further from the mark. They contradicted all the information that we had obtained so far and contradicted one another. It seemed that there was no definite information to be had or that there was an understanding between these officials to keep out intruders at all costs. This theory has become a conviction since then. Why is it that we received contradictory information from all these people unless it was to bewilder us and to dissuade us from going into the forest? As a matter of fact, all of them advised us not to attempt the trip. But we were not to be discouraged so easily.

Then came another bolt from a clear sky.

Although we were merely transient visitors for as short a time as possible, we were told that we would have to pay the full amount of customs duty and the full fee for the use of our rifles—or even for possessing them. Bonded guarantees for the safe return of all the dutiable articles were not suggested until I had shown that no imposition could deter me from entering the Great Forest. I called every bluff, and finally we were told of the best way to achieve our ends.

But again we found that we had been deceived, either intentionally or otherwise. When we arrived at the post where we were supposed to find the best authority (a Beluchistan Indian by the name of Selumani) we found ourselves thwarted again, this time in an almost disastrous manner. We traveled economically and had obtained twenty porters for our luggage. Thinking at the outset that we would reach the forest in three days, we had counted on keeping these porters until our return. But when we found that we had to proceed to a town called Kilo—a matter of five days more marching—the porters left us and would not even come another day's trip with us to Fataki, where we were sure to get other porters. The Indian told us that we should meet up with the White Fathers at Fataki and that they were certain to be able not only to provide us with porters, but to direct us the proper way. We appealed to the local chief, Julu, for porters, but this worthy had not influence enough with his people to get us a guide, not to mention twenty porters. Dr. Shattuck volunteered to leave next morning early to go to the White Fathers and to send back porters to take me and the luggage away from where we were marooned. He started early the next day, and I had just settled down in the afternoon to compose a long article when in walked Dr. Shattuck after a futile march of seven hours and a half, saying that he had completed a circle.

Now it was up to me, footsore and disabled as I was through a festering blister, to take to the road and to make a five-hour journey which turned out to be seven hours. At 8:30 P. M. I finally reached the priests. I was tired, even more footsore and hungry, without any baggage whatsoever, and they gave me all I needed and looked after my torn feet, which pained me sadly. But all the hardships were forgotten when they gave me the glad tidings that I would surely find what I sought in another day's march from Kilo, which is the nearest white settlement to the Mambuti.

The next morning at eight, twenty porters were on their way to Dr. Shattuck, who arrived at Fataki the day after. So here we are to-day, a week after leaving Butyaba, still at the mission of the White Fathers at Fataki, hoping to get away from here to-morrow, on our way to Kilo and the Forest. One thing is accomplished: we have the information which we had tried so hard to get, and there is great probability of seeing the Pigmies. What seems stranger than anything else is that the Fathers can win us an opportunity to film the little fellows, whereas the officials gave us little or no hope of picturing them. The influence of the Fathers over the natives is beyond question far greater than that of the officials.

A striking incident demonstrated this only the day before yesterday. There was an engineer, whom I met at a resthouse of Tsupu, whose porters had run away. He had ordered the local chief to get him twenty porters the next morning. When our porters passed the camp he was still minus porters, and he seized mine as well as the letter I had written to Dr. Shattuck, and these porters were compelled to carry his loads as far as Julu, where Dr. Shattuck was waiting for them. Here, with all his governmental influence, the engineer was unable to obtain other porters to carry him further, but had to send to the nearest headquarters for another lot. The Fathers had no difficulty in getting us porters, not only to go and bring in Dr. Shattuck, but also for our further trip to the forest. "There's a reason."

Now, some one will ask, is the filming of the Pigmies worth all this trouble? More than that! I have made a discovery which so far I have never heard spoken of by any of the authorities whom I have met, nor have I seen any mention of it in any anthropological authorities which I have consulted with regard to the tribes of the Congo. Despite all our mishaps and this long roundabout way to Kilo, I have made this observation: that the tribes which inhabit this district—some 70 miles wide and 140 miles long, between Mahagi and Kilo and between the shores of the Albert Nyanza and a northern branch of the great forest—were gradually decreasing in height as we went along. The Walur, who inhabit the district between Mahagi Port and Mahagi Station and for twenty miles further southwest, are above average size. They are a brother tribe of the Wakavirondo and are of Nilotic origin. They also speak the same language as the Kavirondo. This was my first find and rather a surprise, for there is a distance of some six hundred miles between the two branches, not to mention two lakes, the Kyoga and the Albert Nyanza.

The next tribe bordering on the Walur are called the Walendu, who are purer Nilotic than the Walur, and who are nearly a foot shorter in stature. They are decidedly less intelligent, and altogether below the normal scale of mentality, even as compared with their neighbors, the Walur, who in turn are inferior to their brothers, the Kavirondo. Besides, the Walendu are abnormally cruel in their dealings with each other. Incidents showing this cruelty happen here almost every week. They seem to take a delight in cutting one another's throats and still more in disemboweling their victims at the slightest provocation. The worst of this barbarity is that the culprit flees after the deed and leaves his nearest of male kin to pay for the damage that he has done. It is the custom of these natives to seize the brother, who may be absolutely innocent of his kinsman's crime, and to visit on him the same affliction which the criminal has visited on his victim. The language of the Walendu is still a greater manifestation of their low intellect. It is a language of monosyllables without a trace of syntax, articles or even pronouns. One word or syllable has from five to ten different meanings, distinguished from one another only by a variation of intonation and accent. Genders are unknown in this tongue, nor is there declension of nouns or conjugation of verbs. It is said that there is a similar language to be found in the Soudan, and hence some maintain that the Walendu are originally from the Soudan. But the lower jaws of these strange natives are so prominent and protruding that they could scarcely claim relationship with those tribes whose lower jaws are distinctly recessive. Moreover, the Soudanese are not of short stature. However, this is a question for an anthropologist of authority to decide, and I would merely suggest that here is a field open for investigation for the ethnologist which will reveal new and wonderfully interesting material.

The next tribe to the southwest of the Walendu is another race entirely—the Wanyari, which belongs to the Bantu family, and which is again a grade shorter than the Walendu. There are, therefore, within a

HOME BREWING IN UGANDA
Beer made of ripe bananas

A MUBIRA WOMAN WITH A DISC LIP (CONGO)

When the lipdisc is removed the feature is very ugly. Mubira woman of the Congo with lipdisc inserted. Profile showing two and one half inch lipdisc.

radius of 140 miles, four different tribes, each
of them decreasing in stature as they come
nearer to the great forest—the Walur, the
Walendu, the Wanyari, and finally the Mambuti. The picture shows four good types of
these taken from a mixed congregation of
1,200 people at the Mission of Kilo. I was
careful to include no extremes except the
Mambuti, who was the only one there and
rather tall among his tribesmen. None of
these tribes is very numerous in population,
for there are only 60,000 Walendu and 12,000
Wanyari. In their turn the Wanyari are much
smaller than the Walendu, and they attain a
height between the Walendu and the Pigmies.
They are not all of the same stature, but their
average length would probably be four feet
and a half.

The strange feature is that there is
quite a sprinkling of taller people among
them, and this would logically suggest that
they are a mixture of Pigmies and Bantu.
And yet this is not in accordance with some
facts which are known of old. For instance,
there is a tradition which claims that the Pigmies and the Wanyari traded with one another
in a most original fashion. The Wanyari
would bring their products, such as salt,

bananas and other commodities, to a certain
spot on a certain set date of the month, and
the Pigmies would come the day after or during the night, when the Wanyari had retired
to their villages. The little men then would
select what they needed or fancied and leave
their goods, such as ivory and forest products,
for the Wanyari to take away the next day.
This would seem to exclude the idea of inter-
breeding between them in days gone by.

There is another striking difference between the races on the east shores of the lakes
and those on the west. While there is a great
reverence among the peasants for the chiefs
and the kings even in so sophisticated a tribe
as the Baganda, that characteristic is absolutely lacking among their western brother
tribes. The chiefs of the Walur, the Walendu
and the Wanyari have no power whatsoever
over their subjects. Each native seems to be
his own chief here. Whether this is owing to
the lack of government on the part of the Belgians or an ancient custom seems to be a
mooted question with those who have labored
among them for a number of years. Be this
as it may, the fact remains that when the
white man needs assistance he goes naturally
to the chief. The chief, desirous of making a

good impression, does all that he can to exert
a certain amount of authority over his subjects,
but the results are always nil, as we have discovered again and again when we needed porters. The only man who has any authority
over the natives is the Padri, or "Mopera," as
they fondly call him. He wields his power by
kindness and probably the medicine which he
provides, as well as by the fact that the native
recognizes him as his best friend. Whatever
the cause, here is a phenomenon which is worth
investigating. Whether the Walendu chiefs
ever had the power over life and death as did
the Baganda and other kings and chiefs, or
whether the true patriarchal or monarchial
system has never been known here is a question of great importance. The very fact that
this is so different from the Soudanese system
would argue that these natives never came
from that region.

That, at best, they are a decadent race seems
to be certain. Childbirth is fast decreasing.
Premature births and the consequent deaths
of children are very common and on the increase. Abortive births are as high as twenty-
five per cent. Nor is this the wish of the
mother. Promiscuity or inbreeding are not
the causes. To the contrary, no man can take

as bride a girl who lives in the same village as he. This exclusion is so far-reaching that when a girl lives in a village where the prospective bridegroom has a relative the proposed match is *ipso facto* nullified. This tendency is so pronounced that the clergy of the Catholic Church are not at all concerned about the danger of consanguinity for the very reason that the natives themselves have great horror of such unions. What, then, can be the reason? Although the extinction of the tribes would not be a great loss to civilization or to the human race, this is a question well worth studying, even if humanitarian considerations were excluded.

A people of so many vices and so few virtues would be no loss to the world, but we may learn from them lessons which might be applied profitably to our own conditions. It is strange to find the same complaint here as we found in the east, although there the cases are more pronounced and easily traceable. I am told that statistics even of the Kavirondo, who seemed so prolific a tribe, show that there is a tremendous margin on the wrong side between the death rate and the birth rate. Some tribes have only themselves to blame, promiscuity being the great evil among all of them. But why should this same condition exist where promiscuity is frowned upon and actually abstained from? The Wanyari have lost recently more than 800 through meningitis, 1,100 through Spanish influenza, and 700 through smallpox. The Mambuti were reduced by 50 per cent through influenza.

There is one other very pronounced fact which stares one in the face when reaching the Congo and traveling through its vastnesses. The beginning of the administration of the Congo by the Belgians and that of the British in East Africa and Uganda is about contemporaneous, but observe the difference in results. Belgium has taken out treasures and given nothing in return. England has paid out money and fortunes and is still looking for returns; but traveling in Uganda and British East Africa is a pleasure; in the Congo it is a hardship. The British government stations, the roads, railways, the steamers, the opening of the country to settlers, all indicate so superior an administration that no comparison can be made. The British seem to delight in making the countries under their protectorates a civilized world from the outset, whereas the Belgians do not care so long as there is a good margin of revenue to be had.

The schools, soldiers, police and educational institutions of the Belgians are prominent through their absence, except where the missionaries have taken up the work. The clothing of their askaries (native soldiers and police), and especially of the natives in the villages, is the best sign of the total absence of pride in the tribes which they govern. Their soldiers are ragged in the extreme, and they seem to be possessed of the same spirit of graft which their masters exhibit wherever and whenever they come in contact with a victim whom they can hold up. For example I shall quote only a question of exchange. We had to get francs because rupees were not legal tender here. The actual exchange is seven francs for the rupee, when you wish to convert francs into rupees, but when you wish to get francs they offer you three for the rupee. So they have you coming and going. Even the Indian traders are not quite such Shylocks as the government officials. I had an exchange from them at the rate of four francs to the rupee. It is the same with customs duty. Whether they delight in harassing the Americans or whether they wish to keep them out of their country for fear of unpleasant publicity, who shall say?

MAKING REED DOORS IN UGANDA
The background is a royal fence made of the same material

ROYAL FENCE AROUND THE KING'S ENCLOSURE

As I said before, the Belgian Government
works the country for all available resources
and gives nothing in return. For instance,
there are the Kilo gold mines. There are four
mining districts in the Kilo territory, and between them they produce something like
20,000,000 francs per annum. With a little
more organization they could treble the out-
put, but native labor is so scarce and the natives
are so much left to their own devices that the
officials cannot get more black labor to assist
them. Now in this same territory the roads
are in so abominable a condition that travel
is almost impossible. The roads cannot even
be utilized for a bicycle; a motorcycle is entirely out of the question. To make matters
even worse, the question of exchange is not
at all affected in this territory for the reason
that gold, which was formerly worth three
francs and a half the gram, commands now
more than twenty. It would be imagined that
since gold has gone up in price as well as exchange, the gold produced here would be
utilized for the expansion of the country or for
the purchase of goods and necessary commodities, but nothing of the kind is happening.
The commodities which formerly were ordered
from Nairobi in British East Africa are no

longer ordered there, nominally because the exchange of the rupee is too high. As a matter of fact, such is not the case. Their gold is worth more now at present exchange rates than it was in normal times, and gold would buy more now than it did then. Do they take advantage of this for the benefit of the country? No; the gold is shipped home and the country is drained of the necessities of life to such an extent that at the time of writing it is impossible to buy sugar, petrol, canned goods of any description, cloth, candles or other staples. Even the officials have to go without all these things, which are absolute necessities for the barest comfort.

The officials are paid at the present rate of exchange and the franc does not buy them a fourth of what it did formerly. It is not strange, therefore, that the officials are hopelessly inefficient. This fact is so potent that the government cannot even induce Belgians to take these posts, but employs all manner of adventurers from other nations, such as Greeks and Armenians. That, of course, entails its own drawback and diminishes the respect not only of foreigners but of men of their own country, not to mention that of the natives.

Officials whose names I could mention admit that merchants and heads of commercial houses actually "bum meals" from officials and missionaries because they are not allowed to import from British East Africa and cannot get any supplies from Stanleyville, which is out of reach—45 days' march from Kilo. Officials are the only white men here who have sufficient, and they have no surplus; the White Fathers grow their own staples and are supplied from the headquarters in Uganda. We ourselves could get no tea, no curry, no milk, no petrol, no canned meats, no pickles, or anything needed for our chop box.

There is yet another incongruity which shows that they go from one extreme to the other. About fifteen years ago, 1905-1906, as will be remembered, there was a great outcry against the Belgian atrocities in England and America. Unheard of cruelties were laid at the door of the Belgians, and it does not matter whether or not we took stock in those charges at the time. I, for one, stood up for them and maintained that there were as many cases of mutilation to be found in Uganda as there were in the Congo. It was merely a question of the natives and their old customs, according to which "an eye for an eye and a tooth for a tooth" was the unwritten law. There was, of course, the old tradition among the natives that those in authority had power not only over life and death, but also the right to mutilate—a common practice. The Belgians were no more to be blamed for those mutilations in the Congo than the British were for those in Uganda.

However, that is old history, and I merely repeat it here to emphasize my proposition that the Belgians reversed their attitude completely. Now it is a question of laxity and neglect rather than one of harshness. The regulations for the officials are such at the present writing—1920—that under no circumstances or provocation may they use the lash. Even to shoot a gun from a distance as a warning when there is trouble is forbidden because it means a menace to the native. When an official slaps a native in the face for insubordination or for any other cause he is sent to. jail for four days and imprisonment means revocation of his commission and dismissal from the service. All of these measures are taken to pacify their critics, who assailed the Belgians on the score of atrocities in former days.

This, I maintain, is an absurd situation

in which the one extreme is worse than the
first, and in which the remedy is worse than
the disease. It shows a weakness in the government which not only works harm to the
native but which militates against any chances
of establishing good government and order in
the future. So marked is the lack of government that the vices of the natives will never
be stamped out under the present régime.
Take, for instance, the cruelty of the Walendu,
who, as I have mentioned, cut one another up
on the slightest provocation, or lack of it. The
officials permit the natives to take the law into
their own hands and to punish an innocent
person, such as the nearest relative or brother
of the criminal. This goes on from year to
year and the first law of colonial government—
to improve native customs where they are detrimental—is obviously ignored.

The improvement in the material aspect of
the country suffers similarly. There is no law
or regulation to enforce labor; taxes are woe-
fully inadequate; education is not even thought
of; public work and industries, good roads, im-
provements in the form of buildings, agriculture and plantations, transportation facilities,
measures for the sanitation of the people,
formation of troops and police, defense for

and protection of the Europeans, commercial
prosperity, even the very elements of civilization, are suffering. I am speaking of the Eastern Congo, especially the Ituria district. The
only "raison d'être" for a colonial or protective
government would be the establishment of
these very essentials, which the officials overlook. To please a critical public or watchful
foreign powers may be a justifiable desire, but
it is altogether out of place to neglect governmental functions in order to placate critics.

If we heard the reason for this wholesale
inefficiency, pronounced once, we heard it at
least a hundred times. That is the fear that
either England or America was anxious to
seize the Congo. And it seemed futile to argue, that we, in America, were not condemn-
ing Belgium for the alleged outrages under
Leopold. As a matter of fact, I believe that
the ostensible explanation was merely a lame
excuse for the present policy of listless "laissez
faire," and a poor apology for the present
lackadaisical and negligent régime. The expressions of suspicion of the British Government of Uganda and British East Africa and
the Anglophobic fear that the English are only
waiting to annex this country are absurd.
More than once we were asked whether the

American Government had no intentions of taking over the Congo. And it seemed not to pacify them at all when we asserted that the United States did not entertain any imperial aspirations whatsoever.

That seems to be the bugbear and the great fear among all of the officials. And to a great extent I believe that this is at the bottom of their present policy of keeping down expenses and of taking all out of the country without putting anything into it. The possibilities are no doubt enormous and if this country were made to yield according to its resources and capabilities by a systematic process which worked mutually for the benefit of the governors and the governed, there is not the slightest doubt that this territory would be a winner in a very short time, a land able to show a profit that might even help to pay off Belgium's national debt. But to take all and return nothing is a policy that will antagonize other nations, and if the Belgians cannot be induced to mend matters the Congo should be taken out of their hands or a trustee appointed to see that they administer it properly.

How often did we say to one another that if the United States had this country what a vast difference it would make in a very short time. Turn loose a few American engineers in these vastnesses and the railroads would be carrying ivory, gold, rubber and coffee in such quantities as to flood the markets of the world, and American prosperity would make the Congolese smile from ear to ear as well as make them a happy people instead of the stooping, resentful and totally uncivilized and ragged "niggers" that they are now.

I am told that the epidemics in this country are worse than in any other known native district. One seems to follow the other. Smallpox, sleeping sickness, plague, cholera, meningitis and famine follow each other in rapid succession, and now a new disease has broken out to which no name has yet been given. I was told by the official of Djugu that he had found that a whole village had died of a complaint, the symptoms of which were a continual hemorrhage from the lungs for two days, followed quickly by death. Not a patient recovered after the first hemorrhage had seized him, and of a village of more than 200 people there is not one survivor. So far it has not spread to any other village, but a report had been sent to the District Medical Officer.

The Pigmies, or Mambuti, as they call them-

MAMBUTI (PIGMY) FAMILY REUNION IN FRONT OF THE
ANCESTRAL PALACE

A MAMBUTI (PIGMY) ARCHER

selves, and as the other native tribes in the
Congo call them, claim to be the oldest race
in the eastern part of the Congo. Originally
they had a free hand in this country and
roamed about as they pleased, occupying a
stretch of open land now and then, or retiring
to the forest, as the spirit moved them. They
resented the settlement of the Wanyari in their
territory to such an extent that even now they
kill the Wanyari whenever they feel so inclined
if intruders dare to enter the domains of the
Pigmy forest. This they do only by sniping,
because they dare not fight their foe in the
open, where they know that they would not be
the equal to the Wanyari. They lie in wait for
them in the forest, and from ambush it is an
easy matter, comparatively, to land one of
their poisoned arrows in the anatomy of their
hated enemies.

At present, however, the Pigmies are
not, as a race, quite so hostile to the
Wanyari. They have taken their ejection
philosophically for the past half century, and
now they not only look upon the Wanyari as
a race of conquerors, but almost as friends in
general. But they do not soon forget a personal slight or injustice; hence occasional
vendettas. The Wanyari on their side do not

make such cases of revenge a "casus belli," well knowing that it would be futile for them to pursue the Pigmies into their native haunts, the forest. There the Pigmies are monarchs of all they survey, and they can live in the forest until further orders; indeed, it is their instinct.

They live as close to the monkey as it is possible for human beings to do. They eat the produce of the forest; they shelter under trees and boughs; they make huts of the twigs and leaves of the forest; they need no open space or sunshine; and they are as happy without cover or shelter as they are under it.

Who shall dare to attempt to give a history of their origin or even a reason for their undersized stature? Theories have been advanced by the dozens, and although they doubtless have a certain amount of foundation on scientific and physical grounds, other peoples have lived under the same conditions and thrived. Consider, for instance, the Algonquins and the Mohawks in the vast forests of North America. They lived in the dark recesses of the forests, they hunted under the branches of the trees, hid for protection, shrunk to shield themselves against the low-hanging boughs and foliage of

the ubiquitous forest growth. They avoided
the saplings which seem to affect their muscles
and nerves. They rarely saw the sun and felt
as much at home sleeping on the pine needles
as do the Pigmies on and under the leaves.

The French Canadian is one of the giant
specimens of the extreme north of the American continent. True, he lives in a different and
colder climate, while the Pigmy lives on the
Equator. But nevertheless an analogy refutes
the idea that it is the darkness of the forest
and the continual bowing under the branches
of the trees that makes them what they are—
the smallest race of the human family.

Lack of sunlight and prowling about in a
stooping position are the most forceful argument for their size, in my estimation. Food
conditions are another; but there are other
races who are principally vegetarians and one
could scarcely call the Pigmies vegetarians
pure and simple. They live by their arrows
as well as by the fruits of trees and roots.
There would, therefore, be more reason for the
Indians in Asiatic countries to be diminutive
in size than for the Pigmies.

Another favorite theory of mine was ex-
ploded with an equally loud detonation. I
had always advanced the hypothesis that the

negroes were black chiefly on account of the
unmerciful sun which shone upon them from
the cradle to the grave. But although the
Pigmy is somewhat lighter of complexion than
the negro, there are more black Pigmies than
there are yellow. And, strange to say, the
light color seems to run more among the
women than the men, although I have not seen
enough of them to postulate this as a fact. In
the two villages which we entered we saw sixty-
five in all, but they were the average Pigmy,
and some of them true types and small enough,
as can be seen by the pictures we took of them.
Even the lighter complexioned ones among
them are dark enough to be classed among the
negroes, if color were the criterion. Here,
then, goes my favorite notion that eternal sunshine makes negroes black, because the Pigmies
can under no stretch of imagination be said to
be living under the rays of the sun.

There is very little to say about the Pigmies,
and although they are, as it were, a freak of
nature and draw the attention of the world
by their low stature they are disappointing
when one has taken the trouble to march 200
miles to see them. They are clannish and live
among themselves without caring to mingle
with the rest of mankind. Even those who

live on the fringes of the great Congo forest mix very little with the tribes immediately surrounding them. Some of the chiefs of the Wanyari have, so to speak, adopted them, and they are welcome in Wanyari villages, but even here the Mambuti prefer to have their own villages in the neighboring forest and emerge only occasionally to obtain a square meal and they return to their haunts as soon as possible.

Nor have they their fixed abodes. They never linger longer than a fortnight in their villages, which are as diminutive as their bodies. They cut a few branches, bend them with both ends in the soil and gather enough leaves to secure a cover without bothering about protection against the rains or leaks. There is no particular shape or architecture which they follow, and they seem satisfied to have their huts oval or in the form of a bread loaf or beehive.

As with the Masai, the women do the construction and the men do not lift a hand to aid them. The women select the boughs and collect the leaves for the awnings. It takes very little time, as the material is right at hand wherever they go. They live there for only two weeks at the longest—then they move again to more productive regions, because they do not care to go far for a livelihood, and naturally the birds of the forest are soon scared away by their arrows and the eatable roots and fruits of the trees are soon exhausted. The small game are driven out by their arrival and there remains little to eat; consequently the Pigmies also move away from so inhospitable a place.

There is another reason for which they leave a location, and that is the killing of a Wanyari or other tribesman. Then they move fast and farther for fear of being caught. They leave few or no trails, because they are so small and light and used to travel in the forest that they scarcely leave a footprint. They have no baggage to remove and they never have any set trails on which they go about. The principle of the line of least resistance is understood better by this little gentry than by any other set of men, because they circle around a thickly brushed area to gain a few feet on their way. They naturally avoid swamps and rivers in the forest because they could not wade in deeply, and wherever necessary they jump from cluster to cluster of papyrus or other swamp vegetation.

When pursued by an animal which is

AFRICAN PERAMBULATORS

Mother knows how to give it comfort   Sister takes care of baby after a manner

TWO EMBU BELLES
Notice similarity to the Wakikuyu girls

too large for their arrow and too dangerously quick on its feet, they climb a tree and follow the principle of "watchful waiting," although they have never even heard of the existence of the author of the expression. This is a favorite ruse when they happen on the trail of an elephant. When this occurs, the whole tribe moves and follows its scouts for days and days. They pepper the big brute with their arrows and put their spears in the branches of the trees so they will pierce the back of the huge prey until it finally is exhausted or dies of loss of blood. In this case they call in the neighboring Pigmy settlements, and when finally the trunked mass falls down, they climb on top of it in swarms like ants over a bug.

Such a day is a red letter day for the little men and they feast on the elephant carcass for weeks. They usually point out the tusks to a friendly Wanyari chief in their neighborhood, who sells them for the Pigmies at the best price offered. They naturally do not ask for the value in money, because they would not know what to do with coin, but they sell it for salt and tobacco and some arrowheads or spears included in the bargain. It is particularly puzzling how they can kill so large an animal with their little arrows and with their little bows. These articles of defense and attack look more like the toys of our children than like the formidable weapons which they are in the hands of these miniature men. Their spears also are in proportion to their size, and there are few of these.

Withal, it is a mystery to me how they can live except, as one official explained it, that they are the nearest expressions of humans living reduced to the fundamental requirements of life's sustenance. They do, as a matter of fact, live little beyond or above the monkeys.

The Pigmies are a Nuba race, or, as some define them, of the Bushman genus. They have probably preserved their national customs better than any other race because they have so few, and because of their size they have little or no opportunity to intermarry and to ally themselves with other races. The strangest feature about them is that they are monogamous. There is little danger of inbreeding, because every one knows who is who, and why. Consequently there is no degeneration of the breed and monogamy reduces venereal disease to a minimum. At present there is a slight tendency for them to consort with the Wanyari because the extremes of the two races are close

together, so far as size is concerned; the shortest specimens of the Wanyari being approximately of the same height as the tallest of the
Pigmies. But even here there are very few
cases of close alliances.

The odd part of it is that in such cases the
Mambuti, or Pigmy, women discard their native objections to competitors in the affections
of their spouses. They are glad to become
number two or even the third factor in the
husband's connubial establishment. Those
whom I have seen seemed to be glad to get
away from the forest and to enjoy God's own
sunshine. And so, at least for that one day,
did the population of a whole village which
we took out of their native surroundings in
order more easily to take pictures of them,
which was a hopeless case in their own environ-
ments. They all seemed to enjoy the sun, and
they danced in it to their hearts' content until
the perspiration was gushing down their little
limbs.

Why, one asks, do they not escape their captivity in the forest? That is a hard question
to answer. It may be on account of their innate objection to work. They live like the
creeping things in the woods. They neither
sow nor harvest. There was not a hoe to be

found in the possession of any native of the two villages we encountered. Theirs are not the worries of trades or industry. No agricultural instincts are to be found in their little souls. Solomon's glory of wealth and raiment has no attraction for them, and their babies are well cared for when they have forest leaves or sometimes a soft and shady banana leaf to cover them from exposure to the elements. What more would they want? Even the latter luxuries are borrowed from their more fortunate brethren of the surrounding villages of the Wanyari.

Whenever we saw them dance their primitive passes they seemed to be a supremely happy crowd. The songs accompanying their dance were a monotonous yodel without any words— mere sounds. The women yodeled the chorus while the men sang the drone. What they seemed to enjoy especially was the open space in the village, where they were the guests of the chief; it was so smooth to dance on and so wide—and they were used only to a narrow, rough space between their little huts. The women ran around making all sorts of grimaces. They were drunk with delight; they swayed from side to side with fatigue until they were ready to drop from sheer exhaustion. Children around the Maypole never had a better time; even women with children at their breasts joined in the great hilarity.

And what was the reason of it all? Merely the prospect of getting a little salt. Once we had assured them of their safety through the presence of the White Father in charge of the nearest Catholic mission, we could do with them as we pleased. They knew he was their friend, and the chief of the village vouched for our harmless intentions: that was enough for them and they threw themselves wholly into the spirit of the occasion. We photographed them to our hearts' content and they were more docile than any of the tribes we had taken so far. It was a red letter day for them, what with all the bananas and vegetables from the Wanyari gardens and the salt and the tobacco. We offered meat and fowls, but they refused, because they must eat no meat which is not killed by their own hands in the forest. That seemed to be their taboo.

Now why was it that everybody, even to the last party we met on the road in search of them, discouraged us by telling us that we would not find any Mambuti, and that even if we did find them they would run away from us on account of their great timidity? I dislike to draw conclusions, but the fact that the good priest who sponsored us drew them out in great numbers and made them feel so happy speaks volumes as against all the warnings, of officials and merchants alike, that we should fail in our mission.

What struck me as very strange in these Mambuti is the fact that notwithstanding their savage surroundings and the extremely low ebb of their mentality and culture that they should have a faith in one Supreme Being and in a celestial reward after death. Father Buyck, who took the opportunity to give them a religious instruction in the Wanyari language, asked them this question: In how many gods did they believe? And those who understood the question answered with one finger pointing to heaven. They also pointed to heaven when they were asked about the hereafter. The little woman who acted as interpreter put the question to the community and several put up their hands toward the sky and at the same time turned their fingers down to the ground to express their belief that at death part goes up to the sky and part down to earth, which on further investigation was explained by the little woman as a knowledge of the com-

MAMBUTI (PIGMY) MOTHERS IN FRONT OF THEIR FOREST HOME

AMONG THE PIGMIES
Two grizzly old Mambuti (Pigmy) hunters
Three Mambuti (Pigmy) males of the younger set

posite make-up of the human being of soul
and body. This she further emphasized by
mentioning the haunting ghosts of the forest.
At the mention of this fact, which for further
information she put up to the little men, they
nodded as if in confirmation of what she had
explained to Father Buyck in the Wanyari
language. They looked at the good priest with
a sly fear in their eyes, as if he might have the
power of communication with these spirits.
This happened at the Zabu village, where we
found 26 Mambuti. It must be remembered
that we had a little stray Mambuti woman
who had married a Munyari as an interpreter. She had lived among the Wanyari
so long that she may be considered to have
been under the influence of the Wanyari partial acceptance of Christianity, especially because Zabu himself was a Catholic. This
became all the more apparent when we made
the same investigation in the next village,
where the result of our researches were totally
different.

In the next village, where there was a
gathering of over forty Mambuti, the
question of their belief in a Supreme Being
was met with a total blank stare, as if

they did not understand what was being talked about. And since I was particularly anxious to have this question decided, the question was put again and again in different forms, but the blank stare was as often repeated. The little woman put up her hand toward the sky, but there was no indication that the others agreed with her when they were consulted. So evidently the little woman in her dealings with the Wanyari, one of whom she had married, learned of the teachings of the White Father and anxious to please him indicated *her* knowledge rather than that of the Mambuti as a tribe. These answers and their monogamous habits would indicate that they have not been in contact with earlier civilization or with other African tribes, most of which have some idea about a Supreme Being.

What struck me most forcibly was that they are not void of an ethical and moral code. Indeed, the contrast of their ideas of morality with those of other African tribes is so great as to be astounding. It has for some time been a conviction with me that among most of the African tribes, especially those with which I have come in contact, there is almost a complete absence of morality. Homicide, adultery, theft and falsehood, which are the basic vices contrary to the commands of the Decalogue, are considered by most of the tribes as fundamentally opposed to the laws of nature in theory. Tribal laws and customs provide for transgressions in a half-hearted manner. But the observance of such laws are counteracted by a strong and almost general inclination to opportunism in practice. It is an almost general conviction among Europeans of long experience among the tribes of British East Africa and Uganda that to "lie and steal" are a second nature to the natives, one, indeed, in which they take a certain pride. To commit adultery and to kill is considered unlawful; they nevertheless feel no qualms of conscience about such acts. Only exteriorly they are more careful to conceal such facts for fear of reprisal or punishment. They do not boast of such acts among themselves as they do about falsehoods and theft, but as a matter of conscience they do not worry about them.

The sense of morality is stunted, warped or whitewashed, if not totally absent, whatever one may call the phenomenon. It borders on unmorality rather than immorality. The conscious admission of having done a wrong act is lacking in their mental attitude toward such acts. Referring back to the chapter on Kikuyu, the natives of that tribe, which is one of the most advanced in the order of native philosophy, refer to adultery as "stealing," whilst the man who has killed an adversary is looked upon as a hero at a public dance. Among other tribes the latter two breaches of the two first conclusions of the natural law, homicide and adultery, are winked at. Among the Luo or Kavirondo adultery is looked upon with dismay, but rather from a commercial standpoint than a moral one, because "damaged goods" do not fetch the standard price on the matrimonial market. And by the same token, a murderer becomes almost a witch whom all fear and admire and make the recipient of gifts and offerings.

For this reason I was, to say the least, surprised to find the Mambuti imbued with such high moral instincts. Stealing is so foreign to their habits that the Wanyari chiefs give them their goats and sheep to mind whenever a tribe lingers for any length of time in the same locality. This they do because they can rest more easily having their flocks in the hands of the Mambuti than in the hands of men of their own villages. Adultery seems to be almost unheard of among them. That they do not indulge in excesses we found out when they received tobacco and native banana beer from the chief. They drank the beer in moderate quantities and they smoked of the tobacco very frugally.

Their temperance habits were emphasized when we asked the leader of the little dwarfs to pose before us smoking with his pals. He did so, and at the second draft which he took at the pipe, which was as big as himself, he turned over and became fearfully sick, to such an extent that the perspiration gushed down his wrinkled little skin. He was counted out for the rest of the day. That experience also showed us another trait in their character—that they are very sympathetic with one another. As soon as the little man showed a sign of sickness his friends took him out of the sun and laid him in a shaded hut without walls so that he was out of the sunshine and yet exposed to the open air. A little woman, who evidently was his wife, ran for water and plied him with plenty of it, both for drinking and bathing purposes. And when we came to the distribution of salt they took me down to the little invalid and motioned to me not to forget the tiny smoker. I was so gratified with the attention that I gave him a double dose.

Their manners are very gentle and they have a sense of delicacy. I am told also that they do not kill among themselves, and my information went so far as to state that the oldest Mambuti of the two villages with which I came in contact had never known of such an act being committed among themselves. It is true that a couple of Wanyari had become the victims of their poisoned arrows, but they were explained as cases of warfare rather than homicides, because they had intruded into the forest which the dwarfs consider their inviolable domain. In cases where one Mambuti had wounded another with a poisoned arrow they had always applied an antidote in the making of which they are experts.

Their dietetic habits have been alluded to in passing, but it would not be out of place to consider them at somewhat greater length. They live on anything and everything that the forest produces and which is fit for human digestion. Their digestive organs seemed to be developed a great deal better than ours, for they live on roots which would give us dyspepsia for life. I always thought that the African native showed a wonderful digestive system by relishing the raw mohogo or manioc root, but to see the Mambuti eat and gnaw away at roots of the regular forest tree, the name of which is unknown to me, but which seemed a very common species, threw the Wakavirondo and all other husky tribes into the shadow. Nuts and wild fruit in season are, of course, their stock in trade, and they will migrate every now and again to a district where they know such fruit or nuts to be plentiful at the time. Young and tender shoots and "radices" are a delicacy. Fruits, potatoes, vegetables, etc., are indulged in only when they are the guests of the Wanyari chiefs, because they do not cultivate fruits or vegetables of any kind themselves. They have certain herbs which they use for medicine and they are better connoisseurs of the various kinds than an educated botanist. As for meat, they eat only that which the forest supplies and which is killed by themselves or at the killing of which they have assisted and shared in tracking. Birds and small game are staples, with delicacies thrown in, such as elephants, rats, ants and caterpillars. They eat rodents of all kinds, and of these there are many. The rodents' name is legion. I might add that some rodents called Sibili gnaw at an elephant tusk. I noted this habit when a tusk was shown me, the pointed extreme end of which was eaten away by rodents whose teeth marks were visible on the tusk.

A very curious trait of the Mambuti is their courage in the hunting field. It sounds paradoxical that the smallest people known in the human family should have a special predilection in hunting down the largest type of animal life. I shall only mention their hunting methods on gazelle in passing, because as a forest race it is quite natural that they should indulge in trapping whatever is plentiful and secures a good supply of meat. Having no cord or rope, they make their traps and nets of vines and creepers in the form of very coarse and irregular meshes. They place the traps in undergrowth and bushes almost invisible to the watchful gazelle, and having trapped one they kill it with their arrows.

But what is a phenomenal feature in their hunting methods is the long enduring patience which they exhibit in going after elephants, which, needless to say, only happens once in a blue moon.

The fact is, however, that they are clever trackers, and whenever they find a trail of a big tusker they follow it up and the full quota of available hunters is called upon to assist.

FATHER, MOTHER AND GODFATHER

Dr. Vanden Bergh and the shortest Mambuti (Pigmy) family in the village. The husband is four feet four inches tall, the wife is three feet eleven inches.

WOMAN CARRYING HER YEAR'S RESULT OF
COPRA ROPE MAKING TO THE MARKET

Once they have met up with the elephant they begin to pepper him from all directions from the ground and from the heights of trees out of reach of the long trunk. Their agility in the forest enables them to move quicker than the unwieldy mammoth. They know which way he will turn, being guided by the convenient openings in the thick arborage which their colossal prey naturally would look for.

One party keeps up the fight with arrows whilst another detachment plants the available spears overhead in the branches forming a natural arch under which the pursued animal is likely to pass. The spears are fixed head down with the intention to lodge near the shoulders, where they will do most harm near the heart. Once the spear sticks its point is driven farther into the huge body until it sometimes reaches a vital spot. I am told that they also use poisoned arrows which will kill the elephant without affecting the meat for consumption.

They stay with their victim for weeks, until finally the great monster collapses through exhaustion or owing to a fatal wound. Once he is down they finish him in short order and call the balance of the tribe together for the big barbecue. They feast on its carcass, climbing all over him like a swarm of ants, tearing away at the best parts of the meat in great glee until there is little left of the mountain of viands.

The tusks are hidden until they can dispose of them to the Wanyari or Walendu chiefs, who pay them in arrows, spears, salt and tobacco. I have an idea that these sly gentry, who make enormous profits on the transaction, keep the Mambuti away from contact with white men, Indians and Arab traders because the source of profit is too tempting to have it exposed to a direct and open market. For this reason they tell the Mambuti that the white man is very dangerous to meet, whilst they hold off the white man by maintaining that the Mambuti are so timid that they plunge deeper into the recesses of the vast forest whenever a white man is in the neighborhood. In fact, I entertained a Belgian trader in Zabu's village who had been in the district for a number of years and had only seen two Mambuti on the road, who immediately dived into the forest when they saw him. Zabu, the chief, also treated the trader with scant courtesy and looked suspicious when he found the man sitting at our table. He evidently was afraid that we might introduce him to the Mambuti.

The Mambuti, although they are very small in size, are very well proportioned and physically very fit. Whereas they lack the avoirdupois of the larger negro and the brute strength of their better developed brothers, their endurance and muscular development are remarkable. I have seen women of one meter and twenty centimeters carry away a bunch of bananas which almost reached the ground, suspended from their heads with a leather strap. The men seemed to lift one another with perfect ease, as a wrestler might. To see them is a disappointment, because one would expect some abnormal exhibits of limbs and organs, but they show a proportion which could leave nothing to hope for in perfection.

There are three distinctive features which they all show. The first of these is their hairy and woolly surface, which reaches from their breasts down to the base of the abdomen. Their legs and arms are also over-grown with a plentiful crop of black wiry wool. The second feature is the eye, which has a slant upward almost like the Mongolian type. Their eyelashes and brows derive their slant from the eye, and it makes them look weird and suspicious. Whether or not their vision is affected by the shape of the eye I have not ascertained, but I should fancy it must do so, because their natural position is contracted to such an extent that the pupils are thrown out of line. The third and the most appalling feature is their upper jaw. This feature is almost apelike. The upper lip is stretched almost to a bursting point over their prominent jaw and upper row of teeth. The mouth is wide and reaches almost to the center of their cheeks, giving their face in profile a monkeyish expression. The receding nose emphasizes this feature through its almost flat appearance, with widely extended nostrils. The upper jawbone stands out like a round façade, protruding over the under jaw, and to perfect the apish appearance their foreheads are low and slanting in the extreme. It spoils the effect of the well-shaped body entirely, and were it not for that splendidly formed miniature human body one would imagine that their protoparent, at least, was allied to the monkey. Another feature which is, however, not general enough to make it an essential characteristic, is the light complexion, especially of the women. Nevertheless, I should say that 50 per cent are as dark as the average negro.

Their height ranges from one meter, eighteen centimeters, to one meter, thirty-five. Among the women there seems to be an unusual breast development, which begins at an early age. One might mention the large, almost unproportioned size of their buttocks, which was noticeable among the specimens we saw. That also seemed to be more pronounced among the women than the men. However, this is not so prominent a variation from the ordinary negro as might be imagined. I believe that most of the black races have this in common, and I would think that it is probably a result of carrying children and loads of food, water and fuel, a burden which bends their spines in order to keep a balancing position when they are marching. Sometimes they bear this double load for hours and for days. In some cases a load is so great that one would fear inward curvature of the spine. The top of the head of the Mambuti is almost flat, more so among the women than the men. This might be explained by the receding forehead, which has little curve to offset the line of demarcation between the forehead and the upper skull, yet the lack of the sudden curve of the forehead gives them a distinctly flat-headed appearance, which only a full crop of hair may give a different look.

Among those who had their heads shaven lately the flat effect suggested itself most strikingly.

Their minds seem to be proportioned to their bodies. Their mental development keeps pace with their low stature. That, in particular, seems to be the cause of their lack of desire and absence of intention to ameliorate their condition in life. Socially they have no aspirations, and the fact that they are so small and insignificant appears to affect their dealings with other men and tribes. They even look upon the Wanyari, who are their superiors in height only by a few inches, as almost perfect types of men. They quickly assume an inferior position to any tribe which happens to surround them or to border on their frontiers. Upon these neighbors they depend for their trading, and to them they go for exchange of food in return for their ivory. In this case they hide the ivory which they have accumulated in the trunks of fallen trees, and when they need food they make a bargain, of which the other party always gets the benefit. They seem to look upon the other tribe as their patron, if not protector, when they go out into the world or to seek the society of other tribes.

BAGANDA ARE VERY CLEVER AT MAKING OF THE "LUBUGS" BARKCLOTH

The bark is stripped from the Matuba tree and beaten with the mallet until it stretches
out to a length of twelve feet and breadth of ten feet

BAGANDA WOMEN ARE CLEVER MAT WEAVERS
Using shredded palm leaves for material

They may occasionally be seen with a few necklaces, armlets or rings, but these are all from outside markets, and they are principally trinkets discarded by other tribes.

The women sometimes wear amulets for definite purposes. One is the thighbone of a rodent found in the forest. This amulet, when worn by a nursing mother, is a certain guarantee of plenty of milk for the baby. Tails of certain birds are worn by the men for protection against bronchial trouble and pneumonic diseases. For protection against the cold they have only their scanty huts and no clothing whatsoever. During the night they cuddle together on the unyielding ground and pile on top of one another to obtain a certain amount of warmth. They have large families. I saw one family of four children and spoke with a mother who had raised nine. They have great respect for their elders, and in this connection I noticed that a girl whom I pushed ahead to lead a dance withdrew, made place for the oldest woman in the party, and took her own place near the rear of the line. The same rank was in order with the men, the oldest always in the lead, and when he fell out another gray-haired elder took his place. When we

went to their forest home a young woodsman
led the way, but he withdrew in favor of the
oldest in the village, who led us on and found
the intricate path which wound its way to their
abode.

THE END